TEACHER'S EDITION

Jazz Chants

FOR CHILDREN

CAROLYN GRAHAM

Illustrations by Anna Veltfort

OXFORD UNIVERSITY PRESS

Oxford University Press

200 Madison Avenue
New York, N.Y. 10016 USA

Walton Street
Oxford OX2 6DP England

OXFORD is a trademark of Oxford University Press

Library of Congress Cataloging in Publication Data

Graham, Carolyn.
Jazz chants for children.

SUMMARY: A collection of chants, songs, and poems designed
to teach the rhythms of spoken American English primarily
to students of English as a second language.

1. English language—Text-books for foreigners.
2. English language—Spoken English—Juvenile
literature.   3. Children's songs—Texts.
4. Children's poetry.   [1. English language—
Textbooks for foreigners]   I. Title.
PE1128.G65   784'.3   78-11858
ISBN 0-19-502497-4

Printing (last digit): 20 19 18 17 16 15 14 13 12

Printed in the United States of America.

Jazz Chants® is a registered trademark of Oxford University Press

4211289

Contents

Chants, Songs and Poems:

Page numbers refer to the CHANT GUIDE. The ACTIVITY GUIDE appears on the facing page of each unit.

♪ Musical Notes indicate Songs

What is a Jazz Chant?

JAZZ CHANTS are the rhythmic expression of Standard American English. The Jazz Chants included in this book, and recorded on the accompanying cassette, are designed to teach the natural rhythm, stress, and intonation patterns of conversational American English.

Just as the selection of a particular tempo and beat in jazz may convey powerful and varied emotions, the rhythm, stress, and intonation patterns of the spoken language are essential elements for the expression of feelings and the intent of the speaker. Linking these two dynamic forms has produced an innovative and exciting new approach to language learning.

As a language teaching technique, Jazz Chanting was first developed, by Professor Carolyn Graham, at the American Language Institute of New York University, where it is now an integral part of their language learning program. Oxford University Press published Professor Graham's first book, *JAZZ CHANTS,* for adults and young adults in 1978. Professor Graham began to give workshops to teachers of English throughout the United States, Mexico, Canada, and parts of Europe, demonstrating this technique and explaining how teachers could create their own Jazz Chants. Elementary school teachers in these various workshops encouraged Professor Graham to develop Jazz Chants for children. They realized the potential of this energetic new approach to language acquisition for the elementary school child, particularly because the strong, rhythmic patterns of the chants bear a close relationship to children's games and the child's natural affinity for rhythm and movement.

Carolyn Graham began to work with young children, individually and in groups, in various school systems. The result of those efforts is the present volume, *JAZZ CHANTS FOR CHILDREN.* The Jazz Chants included in this book were especially designed for children. The language is the natural language that children use. The topics and situations of the chants are those which are important to children and which enable them to express in English the many emotions that all children experience. Many of the chants are humorous and also fun to do. Although Jazz Chanting's primary purpose is the improvement of speaking and listening comprehension skills, it also works well in reinforcing specific grammar and pronunciation patterns used in situational contexts relevant to the child's experiences.

Some Preliminary Notes

This volume of JAZZ CHANTS FOR CHILDREN, **Teacher's Edition**, is designed to help you, the elementary school classroom teacher, use Jazz Chants with your students as an exciting and effective tool for English language teaching. The contents of the **Student's Book**, the **Cassette**, and this volume, the **Teacher's Edition**, are described in detail below. In addition, there follow some suggestions for adapting and using Jazz Chants in an actual classroom.

THE STUDENT'S BOOK

The **Student's Book** is designed for children at the elementary school level. In each two-page unit there is a chant, or a song, or a poem on the right-hand page. On the left-hand page there is a picture activity which is directly related, either through topic or structure, to the chant. The picture activities present a task for the children to do, which involves writing in the book. The tasks vary and include connecting the dots, finding hidden pictures or hidden words, spelling puzzles, matching patterns, and coloring the actual pictures.

In the **Student's Book**, a great effort has been made to limit the language of directions necessary to complete the task in the picture activity. This allows the students to work alone, or in groups, with minimal guidance from you. Brown ink is used to indicate examples and sample answers. The directions for the completion of the picture activities are printed in full in the **Teacher's Edition**.

In addition to the written task provided by each picture activity, the pictures themselves provide the stimulus for a variety of other classroom language activities.

THE ACCOMPANYING CASSETTE

Every chant, song, and poem in the **Student's Book** is recorded on a one-hour **Cassette** by the author and a group of young children. Each chant is recorded twice, once by Carolyn Graham alone, then repeated by the author with the children in a choral response.

The first presentation of the chant gives the students an opportunity to listen only. Then, during the second presentation, the students should respond with the children on the tape. The poems are presented by the author alone, and are primarily for listening practice. The songs are also recorded only once, but many of the melodies are well-known and the students should have little trouble joining in, soon after they hear them for the first time.

THE TEACHER'S EDITION

The **Teacher's Edition** consists of the **Student's Book**, presented in reduced page format, an ACTIVITY GUIDE, a CHANT GUIDE, and line space for NOTES to be used by the teacher in individual classroom planning.

THE ACTIVITY GUIDE

The ACTIVITY GUIDE appears alongside the reproduced Activity Page from the **Student's Book**. The ACTIVITY GUIDE presents three different types of suggestions.

TASK

In the **TASK** section of the ACTIVITY GUIDE, directions to be given orally to the students are provided for the completion of every picture activity in the **Student's Book**. The answers, if there are specific answers, for each activity are presented in the **TASK** section.

PRACTICE

The **PRACTICE** section of the ACTIVITY GUIDE provides examples of drills and practice exercises for you to conduct as a reinforcement of the structure presented in the chant or picture activity. These practice activities are an extension of the actual picture activity or the chant presented in the **Student's Book**, and are based on the particular language structure that is part of that unit.

In the **Teacher's Edition** there are usually three or four different suggestions within the **PRACTICE** section. These are graded in difficulty, using a dot system, with one dot being the easiest in language level, two dots being more difficult, and three dots being the most difficult. It is not expected that all the suggestions under **PRACTICE** will be used at the same time with the same group of students. They are for students of varying abilities and should be used at different times according to the individual needs of your students.

In the **PRACTICE** section of the ACTIVITY GUIDE, oral exercises are provided which vary from tightly controlled repetition all the way through free conversation. Oral practice activities include:

- simple repetition
- substitution practice
- listening comprehension practice
- question and answer practice (dialog practice)
- real question and answer practice (where the students actually provide original answers)
- discussion (the least manipulative language practice)

It is important to remember that these practice activities, which occur only in the **Teacher's Edition**, are not complete drills, but simply suggestions of drill types that may be continued by the teacher during classroom practice. In the notation used for these drills, **T** refers to the teacher, **S** refers to all of the students, and **S1**, **S2**, etc. refers to individual students in the class.

ENRICHMENT

The **ENRICHMENT** section of the ACTIVITY GUIDE also occurs only in the **Teacher's Edition**. It provides reinforcement and follow-up of the structure or topic that has already been presented under **TASK** and **PRACTICE**. The **ENRICHMENT** activities are generally suggestions for drawings, games, and puzzles.

THE CHANT GUIDE

The CHANT GUIDE for the **Teacher's Edition** contains detailed suggestions for teaching each chant, song, or poem. The CHANT GUIDE is divided into three sections as follows:

PRONUNCIATION

The **PRONUNCIATION** section of the CHANT GUIDE points out specific sounds that are emphasized in each chant. The CHANT GUIDE also draws attention to the reductions of sound in natural language, such as "Did you eat yet?" becoming reduced in natural conversation to "Jeet yet?" The **PRONUNCIATION** section also points out specific intonation patterns for various structures as they occur in each chant.

STRUCTURE

The **STRUCTURE** section of the CHANT GUIDE emphasizes which structures are taught in each chant and makes generalizations about certain patterns in language with regard to how these patterns occur in each chant.

PRESENTATION

The **PRESENTATION** section of the CHANT GUIDE contains special notes which may be particularly appropriate to the presentation of a chant, song, or poem. General suggestions for presenting chants, songs, and poems are listed below. It should be noted that these are simply suggestions, and you should feel free to experiment and improvise to meet the needs of your own students.

GENERAL SUGGESTIONS FOR PRESENTING THE CHANTS

Step 1   Explain the situational context of the chant, using either the student's native language or very simple English. For example, in the chant **Stop That Noise!** on page 13, you should explain that this chant tells us about the different ways boys and girls ask for quiet, from the very polite to the rude.

Step 2   Have the students listen to the first presentation of the chant on the cassette.

Step 3   Have the students repeat any difficult sounds, or particularly new or difficult structures, which are pointed out in the CHANT GUIDE.

Step 4   Have the students repeat each line of the chant after you.

Step 5   Have the students listen again to the solo presentation of the chant on the cassette.

Step 6   Have the students respond with the group on the cassette.

Step 7   Play the group presentation again, this time dividing the class into two groups, one taking the role of the teacher and one taking the role of the chorus. This provides an opportunity to both ask and answer the dialog of the chant.

SUGGESTIONS FOR PRESENTING THE SONGS

The songs are marked by a musical note ♪ in the table of contents. Play the cassette first, before teaching the words of the song, so the students can hear the melody and rhythm. Generally, the melodies will be familiar to the students. Once the students have listened to the melody on the cassette, have them repeat, preferably with the cassette, each line of the song and then have them sing the entire song through. Have them respond with the group singing on the cassette.

SUGGESTIONS FOR PRESENTING THE POEMS

When presenting a poem, read the poem through once. Then point out any rhyming sounds. Have the students identify the rhyming sounds and repeat them after you. Then, have the students listen to the poem on the cassette. They should then repeat each line after you, in choral repetition. The shorter poems may be memorized and may be assigned to individual students for presentation in class. Also, two students may, in dialog fashion, speak alternate lines of a poem. There are suggestions within the pages of the **Teacher's Edition** for having the students create their own poems.

USING JAZZ CHANTS IN YOUR CLASSROOM

While the chants and the activities teach the basic structures of the English language, they should also be fun to do. The reason they work is that the students like them. They should, therefore, be presented as an enjoyable part of language learning.

Because they teach the basic structures of the language, the chants can be used at any time, with any basal course. If, for example, you are practicing the simple past tense in a basal course, it is very appropriate to change the pace from repetitive drill to a jazz chant and picture activity unit. Jazz chants and the picture activities can be presented as part of a daily lesson for ten minutes a day, or they can be presented for twenty minutes at a time, once a week. You should adapt their use to your needs.

The chants and some of the activities lend themselves to physical games and lots of movement in the classroom. This should be utilized to the fullest extent when possible. They also lend themselves to small group activities; many of these are detailed in the pages of the **Teacher's Edition**.

One last note should be made of the fact that the language on the tape is real conversational English. When words like *gonna* are used, it should be explained to the students that this is the way American English is spoken naturally in casual conversation. However, in written and formal communication, *going to* is retained.

You will find that many of the expressions, particularly the one-word questions and idiomatic phrases, will be learned rapidly and will come out naturally in the students' normal conversation as they develop their English. This is the most welcome and rewarding feature of JAZZ CHANTS FOR CHILDREN.

Structure Key

Structures	Chants, Songs, and Poems	Page

ACTIVITY GUIDE

TASK:

Have the students connect the dots which spell out the words: **HELLO, ERNIE.**

PRACTICE:

● 1. *Where Questions with Contraction*

The questions below are in the singular. Conduct a real question and answer drill in which the answers use *here* (close to the speaker), *there* (farther from the speaker), and *over there* (still farther from the speaker).

T: Where's Ernie?
S: He's here.
T: Where's Tony? (Substitute the actual names of the students.)
S: He's there.
T: Where's Susan?
S: She's over there.

For more advanced groups, introduce the plural with contraction:

T: Where're Alice and Ted?
S: They're over there.

● ● 2. *Vocabulary*

Using the picture of **Ernie** as a reference, introduce vocabulary for various parts of **Ernie's** body and the items of clothing he's wearing. When all appropriate vocabulary is taught, ask the students: ''Where's your _____?'' (nose, shirt, etc.) The student points to the appropriate item.

● ● ● 3. *Yes / No Questions with be and do*

Using the picture of **Ernie** as a reference, conduct a question and answer session using yes / no questions with *be* as well as those with *do.* Have the students answer appropriately.

T: Is Ernie tall?
S: Yes, he is.
T: Is he fat?
S: No, he isn't.
T: Does he wear glasses?
S: No, he doesn't.
T: Do you like him?
S: Yes, I do.

● ● ● 4. Ask students to describe **Ernie** to someone who doesn't know what **Ernie** looks like. This may be expanded to a game where one student describes another, unnamed, student. The class then guesses which student is being described.

Ernie

Say Hello to Ernie: HELLO, ERNIE.

2

ENRICHMENT:

● 1. Have students practice writing their own names. Also, have them write: **hello** and **goodbye.**

● ● 2. *Game: Simon Says*

As an extension of **Practice 2** above, have the students play *Simon Says.* The object of the game is for the students to follow all directions prefaced by the words, *Simon Says,* and to do none of the actions when the teacher *omits* the words, *Simon Says.* For example: ''Simon says, 'Touch your _____.' '' or ''Touch your _____.'' When the game is played rapidly it provides excellent listening comprehension practice.

Ernie

Good morning.
> Hello.

Good morning.
> Hello.

Where's Ernie?
> I don't know.

Where's Ernie?
> I don't know.

Good morning.
> Hello.

Good morning.
> Hello.

Where's Ernie?
> I don't know.
>> Here I am!

It's Ernie! Hello, Ernie.
It's Ernie! Hello, Ernie.
It's Ernie! Hello, Ernie.
It's Ernie! Hello, Ernie.
It's Ernie! Hello, Ernie.
It's Ernie! Hello, Ernie.
It's Ernie! Goodbye, Ernie.
Goodbye, goodbye, goodbye.

3

CHANT GUIDE

PRONUNCIATION:
Practice the pronunciation of **good, morning, hello, know, here** and **goodbye.**

Practice the contractions: **where's, don't** and **it's.**

STRUCTURE:
This song provides practice in the traditional words of greeting and farewell: **Hello** and **Goodbye.** It illustrates the use of the *subject pronoun it* with the contracted form of the verb *be* as it occurs in: **It's Ernie!**

PRESENTATION:
When the students are familiar with the words and melody of this song, you may wish to substitute the students' own names for **Ernie,** adding gestures to accompany the action of the chant, such as waving hello and goodbye.

Listen to the accompanying tape for the melody, tempo and style of presentation of this song.

NOTES

ACTIVITY GUIDE

TASK:
Have the students look at the example in the box. Then have them draw a line from the appropriate part of the body to the correct item of clothing. You may review this orally by asking, or having the students ask, the question:

What do you wear on your _____?

In the word puzzle, have the students circle each hidden word in the boy's shirt and then write these words in the spaces provided, numbered 1 to 10. The hidden words are: **sock, head, hand, hat, girl, boy, glove, his,** and **she.**

PRACTICE:
● 1. *What and Where Questions*
This unit may be used for a listening comprehension exercise contrasting the question words *What* and *Where*. Begin by presenting the question and short answer with the students repeating:

T: What do you wear on your head? A hat.
(Students repeat.)
T: Where do you wear your hat? On my head.
(Students repeat.)

Then have students actually answer the questions.

T: What do you wear on your head?
S: A hat.

Repeat the *What question* several times before switching to the *Where question*.

T: Where do you wear your hat?
S: On my head.

Point out the importance of listening carefully to the first word in the question pattern and illustrate how one simple change alters the entire meaning of the question.

● ● 2. *Vocabulary*
Introduce *prepositions of place:* in, on, under, near, next to, beside and over. These can be used for expansions of answers to *Where questions*. For example: It's *under* the table. It's *next to* the door. Practice these prepositions in the following game.

ENRICHMENT:
● ● 1. *Game*
Have one student hold up an object and ask, "What's this?" A student or the entire class answers. The first student then places the object somewhere in the room and asks, "Where's the _____?" A student or the entire class answers.

Shoes and Socks

What do you wear on your feet?   Shoes.

1. Shoe
2. _____
3. _____
4. _____
5. _____
6. _____
7. _____
8. _____
9. _____
10. _____

4

NOTES

_____

_____

_____

_____

_____

_____

_____

_____

_____

_____

_____

_____

_____

Shoes and Socks

What do you wear on your head?
        A hat.
What do you wear on your hands?
        Gloves.

What do you wear on your feet?
        Socks.
        Shoes and socks.
        Shoes and socks.

What do you wear when it's cold?
        Socks.
        Shoes and socks.
        Shoes and socks.

What do you wear when it's warm?
        Socks.
        Shoes and socks.
        Shoes and socks.

Where do you wear your hat?
        On my head.
Where do you wear your gloves?
        On my hands.
What do you wear on your feet?
        Socks.
        Shoes and socks.
        Shoes and socks.

5

CHANT GUIDE

PRONUNCIATION:
Practice the pronunciation of **what, where, warm, hat, head** and **hands**. Practice the *sh* sound in **shoes** and the contraction, **it's.**

Listen carefully to the reduction in the sound of *do* when it occurs in the questions: **What do you . . . ? Where do you . . . ?**

Listen to the *z* sound of the plural *s* in **hands, gloves, shoes** and the *s* sound of the plural in **socks.**

Notice the reduction in the sound of *and* when it occurs in **shoes and socks.**

STRUCTURE:
This chant provides practice in the *simple present questions* with **What** and **Where**. It illustrates the use of the *possessive adjectives my, your* and the *preposition on* as they occur in: **On my head. On your hands.**

PRESENTATION:
This chant is most effective when presented with a strong underlying beat similar to a military march. The accompanying tape provides a model for the presentation of this chant.

NOTES

ACTIVITY GUIDE

TASK:
Have the students look at the example in the box. Then, while looking at the pictures of the children with their names on their shirts, have the students answer the four questions.

PRACTICE:
Conduct real question and answer drills with the students using the verbs *be* and *do*.

● 1. *Questions with be*

   T: Who is tired?
   S: I am.
   T: Who is hungry?
   S: I am.
   T: Who is thirsty?
   S: She is. (Jane is.)
   T: Who is happy?
   S: We are.

●● 2. *Questions with verbs other than be*

   T: Who has a pencil?
   S: I do.
   T: Who has a pen?
   S: He does. (John does.)
   T: Who likes candy?
   S: We do.
   T: Who likes ice cream?
   S: They do. (John and Jane do.)

●●● 3. *Alphabet Review*
Review the names of the letters of the alphabet. Then teach some simple spellings of classroom objects.

   Review these spellings in a game-like sequence. Point to an object. Have students say it, then spell it. Other students can do the pointing and teams can compete, with each team receiving one point for the correct pronunciation of the object and one point for the correct spelling of the object.

ENRICHMENT:

● 1. *Game: Ghost*
Have students play the game *Ghost*. One student begins to spell a word by giving one letter. For example, an **E.** The next student adds a letter. If a student should give a letter which, by chance, completes the word (**Egg,** for example), that student gets penalized by receiving the first letter of the word *Ghost*. If that same student should complete another word in the game, he receives the second letter of the word *Ghost*. When one student or student team receives the complete word, *Ghost,* the student or team is out of the game.

●● 2. *Game*
Have one student be *It*. That student thinks of an object in the classroom. The student gives the class a clue by telling them one letter of its name. For example: The student says, "I'm thinking of something that ends in **k.**" The other students ask questions about the object and try to guess what it is. Example: "Is it a book?"

Who is Sylvia?

Who has a name that starts with **B?**

Bob does.

1. Who has a name that starts with **M?** _____

2. Who has a name that ends with **E?** _____

3. Who has a name with a **T** in the middle? _____

4. Who has a name with an **L** in the middle? _____

6

NOTES

_____
_____
_____
_____
_____
_____
_____
_____
_____
_____
_____
_____
_____

Who is Sylvia?

Who has a name that starts with **S?**
      I do.
          She does.

What's her name?
          Sylvia.

Who has a name that ends with **A?**
      I do.
          She does.

What's her name?
          Sylvia.

Who has a name with a **V** in the middle?
      I do.
          She does.

What's her name?
          Sylvia.

Who has a name with an **L** in the middle?
      I do.
          She does.

What's her name?
          Sylvia.

Who is Sylvia?
      I am.
          She is.

What's her name?
          SYLVIA!

7

CHANT GUIDE

PRONUNCIATION:
Practice the pronunciation of the final *th* sound in **with**. Notice that the sound of the *wh* in **who** is reduced to *h,* and the sound of *an* is reduced to *n* when it occurs in: **with an L.**
Practice the pronunciation of **name** and **middle.** Practice the contraction, **what's.**

Notice the difference in the pronunciation of the name of the letter **A** and the indefinite article **a.**

Listen carefully to the pronunciation of the third person *s* in **starts** and **ends.**

Listen carefully to the intonation of *information questions* with **Who** and **What** and to the intonation of the *short responses:* **I do. She does.**

STRUCTURE:
This chant provides practice in the *simple present questions* with **Who has, Who is** and **What's** and in the short responses: **I do. I am. She does. She is.**

It also illustrates the use of the *indefinite articles a and an* as they appear in: **a name; a V; an L.**

Notice the use of the expression **in the middle** and the preposition **with.**

Notice that questions with the verb *to have* such as **Who has . . . ?** or **Do you have . . . ?** may also be answered with *have* in the short responses: **I have. Yes, I have.** However, **I do; Yes, I do,** is used more frequently in American English.

PRESENTATION:
This chant may be used to familiarize the students with the pronunciation of the names of the other letters of the alphabet.

Continue the chant by asking the same question type, using individual student's names, such as:

Who has a name that starts with **M?**
Who has a name that ends with **T?**
Who has a name with an **R** in the middle?

NOTES

_____

_____

_____

_____

_____

_____

_____

_____

_____

_____

_____

TASK:

Have the students look at the model pictures of **can't**, **won't**, and **can** in the example box. Then, have them write the appropriate description for each of the pictures below. The answers follow:

1. He can.   2. She can't.
3. She won't.   4. He won't.
5. He can't.   6. She can.

PRACTICE:

Conduct real question and answer drills with the students using the verbs, *can, be, do* and *will* with *short answer responses.*

- 1. *Questions with can and short answer responses*

  T: Can you sing?
  S: Yes, I can.
  T: Can she dance?
  S: Yes, she can.
  T: Can he play the piano?
  S: No, he can't.
  T: Can John read?
  S: Yes, he can.

- 2. *Questions with be and short answer responses*

  T: Is he tall?
  S: Yes, he is.
  T: Are they nice?
  S: No, they aren't.
  T: Is she short?
  S: No, she isn't.
  T: Is she kind?
  S: Yes, she is.

- 3. *Questions with do and short answer responses*

  T: Does he like it?
  S: Yes, he does.
  T: Do you want it?
  S: Yes, I do.
  T: Do they know it?
  S: No, they don't.
  T: Does she see it?
  S: Yes, she does.
  T: Does she want it?
  S: No, she doesn't.

- 4. *Questions with the future will and short answer responses*

  T: Will he do it?
  S: Yes, he will.
  T: Will she go?
  S: Yes, she will.
  T: Will they eat?
  S: No, they won't.
  T: Will she dance?
  S: No, she won't.

  Now combine the sentences above at random, asking students questions with: can / can't, will / won't, is / are, isn't / aren't, do / don't, does / doesn't.

I Love to Say, "I Won't."

He can't.   She won't.   She can.   He can.

1. He can.   2. _____

3. _____   4. _____

5. _____   6. _____

8

ENRICHMENT:

- 1. *Game*

  The students gather in a circle. One student performs an action and asks one of the others, "Can you do this?" If that student can perform the action, he or she does and says, "Yes, I can." If that student performs the action correctly, he then becomes the new leader. If the student cannot imitate the action, he says, "No, I can't." The leader then calls on a different student.

I Love to Say, "I Won't."

I love to say, "I can't."
> I love to say, "I won't."

I love to say, "I'm not."
> I love to say, "I don't."

I love to say, "I will."
> I love to say, "I am."

I love to say, "I do."
> I love to say, "I can."

I love to say, "I won't."
> I don't.

I love to say, "I won't."
> I don't.

Say, "I won't."
> I won't, I won't.
> I won't say, "I won't."
> I won't.

Say, "I can't."
> I can't, I can't.
> I can't say, "I can't."
> I can't.

Yes, you can.
> No, I can't.

Yes, you can.
> No, I can't.

You can do it.
> No, I can't.

Yes, you can.
> No, I can't.

Yes, you can.
Yes, you can.

9

CHANT GUIDE

PRONUNCIATION:
Practice the contractions: **can't, won't, don't, I'm.**
Listen carefully to the pronunciation of **can** and **can't.**

Notice the reduction in the sound of *can* when it appears in the sentence: **You can do it.** Notice that the contraction **I'm** is pronounced as one sound as contrasted with the two distinct sounds of the short response, **I am.**

STRUCTURE:
This chant offers practice in the *simple present tense.* Notice the pattern of the verb followed by the infinitive as in: **I love to say.**

The chant illustrates the use of the *modal auxiliaries,* **can / can't,** to express ability and the use of **will / won't** to express promise and refusal.

Notice the use of the expression, **You can do it!** to offer encouragement, and the use of the *command form:* **Say, "I won't."**

PRESENTATION:
This chant should be performed with lots of feeling. The response, **I won't,** should sound like a strong refusal, and **I can't,** an admission of defeat.

NOTES

_____
_____
_____
_____
_____
_____
_____
_____
_____
_____

ACTIVITY GUIDE

TASK:
Have the students answer the questions using the short response: **Yes, I have.** or **No, I haven't.**

PRACTICE:
- 1. *Vocabulary*
  Teach the vocabulary of food, including breakfast foods, main dishes, snacks and beverages. A list of suggestions follows:

eggs	milk	hamburger
cereal	juice	hot dog
fruit	coffee	chicken
pancakes	tea	fish
toast	soft drinks	steak

- 2. *Habitual Present Tense*
  Conduct a real question and answer drill with the students using the *habitual present tense.*

  T: What do you have for breakfast?
  S: I have eggs.
  T: What do you have for lunch?
  S: I have a hot dog.
  T: What do you have for dinner?
  S: I have a steak.

- 3. *Discussion*
  Have the students discuss the type of food they eat in their country at each of the following events:

birthday party	national holiday
sports event	religious holiday
wedding	

- 4. *Discussion*
  Have the students ask each other questions about food combinations, using the structure: *Have you ever had. . . ?* The food combinations they come up with can lead to interesting class discussions.

ENRICHMENT:
- 1. *Drawing*
  Have the students draw a picture of their favorite food.

- 2. Have the students bring in one kind of food which is a specialty in their country, or have them describe it, pointing out what the food tastes like, looks like, and when it is eaten.

The Hot Dog Song

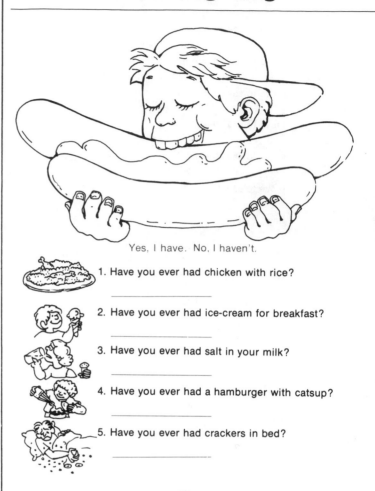

Yes, I have. No, I haven't.

1. Have you ever had chicken with rice?
   _____

2. Have you ever had ice-cream for breakfast?
   _____

3. Have you ever had salt in your milk?
   _____

4. Have you ever had a hamburger with catsup?
   _____

5. Have you ever had crackers in bed?
   _____

10

NOTES

_____
_____
_____
_____
_____
_____
_____
_____
_____
_____
_____
_____
_____

The Hot Dog Song

Have you ever had a hot dog with mustard and mayonnaise?
Have you ever had a hot dog with pepper and salt?
With mustard and mayonnaise
and catsup and pickles.
Have you ever had a hot dog with pepper and salt?

With mustard and mayonnaise
and lettuce and onions
and mustard and mayonnaise
and catsup and pickles
and mustard and mayonnaise
and lettuce and onions
and mustard and mayonnaise
and pepper and salt.

11

CHANT GUIDE

PRONUNCIATION:
Practice the pronunciation of **with.**

Listen carefully to the pronunciation of **hot dog, mustard, mayonnaise, catsup, lettuce, pepper,** and **salt.**

Notice the *z* sound in the plural *s* ending of **pickles** and **onions.**

STRUCTURE:
This song offers practice in the *present perfect tense* when used to express vague, indefinite, past time as in: **Have you ever had . . . ?** Notice that the use of **ever** stretches the time span to include any time in one's life up to the present.

This song also illustrates the plural form of countable and uncountable nouns: **onions, lettuce, pickles** and **catsup.**

Notice that the repeated use of **and** emphasizes the importance of the individual items listed.

PRESENTATION:
The Hot Dog Song is sung to the tune of the traditional folk melody, "Have You Ever Seen a Lassie."

Listen to the accompanying tape for the melody, tempo and style of presentation of this song.

NOTES

ACTIVITY GUIDE

TASK:
Have the students look at the picture and circle each person, animal or thing that is making all that noise.

PRACTICE:
Conduct real question and answer drills with the students using the structures below.

● 1. *Yes / No Questions:* Present Progressive

   T: Is the plane making noise?
   S: Yes, it is. (It's noisy.)
   T: Are the plants making noise?
   S: No, they aren't. (They're quiet.)

●● 2. *Who Questions:* Present Progressive
Ask the class two questions and have them give several answers to each, using either a complete sentence or a conversational short form.

   T: Who's making all that noise?
  S1: The car is (making all that noise).
  S2: The dog is (making all that noise).
  S3: The baby is (making all that noise).
   T: Who's being quiet?
  S1: The cat is (being quiet).
  S2: The sleeping man is (being quiet).

●●● 3. *What Questions:* Present Progressive

   T: What's the dog doing?
   S: He's barking.
   T: What's the taxi driver doing?
   S: He's shouting (yelling, screaming) at the dog.

ENRICHMENT:

● 1. *Discussion*
Have the students discuss and / or draw different examples, from their own experiences, of people or things that are noisy and those that are quiet.

●●● 2. *Role Play*
Have the students act out a skit in which one student is trying to read or listen to music while another student starts to make noise. Introduce words and expressions appropriate to the situation such as: Please be quiet. Stop that noise! I can't sleep.

Stop That Noise!

WHO'S MAKING ALL THAT NOISE?

12

NOTES

Stop That Noise!

Teacher:	Sh! Sh! Stop that noise!
Chorus:	Sh! Sh! Stop that noise! Sh! Sh! Stop that noise!
Teacher:	Come on girls, tell all the boys. Tell all the boys to stop that noise!
Girls:	Please be quiet. Stop that noise! Please be quiet. Stop that noise! Please be quiet. Stop that noise!
Teacher:	Come on boys, tell all the girls. Tell all the girls to stop that noise!
Boys:	Shut up girls! Stop that noise! Shut up girls! Stop that noise! Shut up girls! Stop that noise!
Teacher:	Come on girls, come on boys. Tell everybody to stop that noise!
Chorus:	Sh! Sh! Stop that noise! Sh! Sh! Stop that noise! Sh! Sh! Stop that noise!
Teacher:	Tell all the boys to stop that noise!

13

CHANT GUIDE

PRONUNCIATION:
Practice the pronunciation of: **Sh!, please, quiet, all, that, noise.**

Listen carefully to the pronunciation of the *st* in **stop.**

Notice the *th* sound in **that** and the *z* sound in the ending of **noise** and **boys.**

STRUCTURE:
This chant provides practice in the *command forms* using *stop,* as it occurs in **Stop that noise!** and *tell,* as it occurs in **Tell all the boys.**

It also illustrates several ways to complain about noise from the polite, gentle, **Sh! Please be quiet;** to the angry, rude, **Shut up!**

Notice the use of the *definite article the* as it occurs in: **the boys; the girls.**

PRESENTATION:
This chant can be introduced by asking the students what they say when someone is making too much noise. Their answers may be written on the blackboard, including **Sh! Please be quiet** and **Shut up!** Indicate which are the polite forms and which forms would be considered rude.

NOTES

ACTIVITY GUIDE

TASK:
Have the students circle the twelve hidden beetles in the picture.

PRACTICE:
- 1. *Present Tense to Past Tense*

  Have the students transform your sentences to the *simple past tense.*

  T: He looks at me.
  S: Yesterday, he looked at me.
  T: I see a beetle.
  S: Yesterday, I saw a beetle.
  T: She smells the flower.
  S: Yesterday, she smelled the flower.
  T: He plays with the bug.
  S: Yesterday, he played with the bug.

- 2. *Vocabulary*

  Introduce vocabulary appropriate to the outdoors and particularly to this picture.

grass	flower
tree	frog
beetle	goat
butterfly	leaf
caterpillar	leaves

- 3. Ask the students to describe the picture on the Activity Page. They should tell what is in the picture and where the various items are located.

ENRICHMENT:
- 1. *Discussion*

  Have the students discuss one event, using the *simple past.* Examples: Yesterday, I saw a dog. Yesterday, I went to the movies.

- 2. *Drawing*

  Have the students draw pictures containing hidden objects. Have them exchange the pictures with their neighbors and try to find the hidden objects.

I Saw a Little Beetle in the Kitchen Sink

Circle 12 hidden beetles.

14

NOTES

_____

_____

_____

_____

_____

_____

_____

_____

_____

_____

_____

_____

_____

_____

_____

I Saw a Little Beetle in the Kitchen Sink

I saw a little beetle in the kitchen sink.
I saw his baby brother on the floor.
I saw his great big father near the windowpane.
I hope I don't see them anymore.

I saw a little beetle in the kitchen sink.
He was playing with his brother.
I looked at him.
He looked at me.
We were both scared of each other.

15

CHANT GUIDE

PRONUNCIATION:
Practice the pronunciation of **little, beetle,** and the contraction **don't.**

Listen carefully to the *ch* sound in **each, kitchen;** the *th* sound in **brother, father, other;** and the final *th* sound in **both.**

Listen to the *t* sound in the final past tense ending of **looked.**

Notice the reduction in the sound of *them* and *at* when they occur in the sentences: **I hope I don't see them anymore. I looked at him.**

STRUCTURE:
This poem illustrates the use of the *simple past tense statement* with regular and irregular verbs: **looked, saw, was, were;** contrasted with the *past continuous statement,* **He was playing . . .** Notice that the *past continuous tense* provides a descriptive background for the more immediate and important action of the *simple past:* **I looked at him. He looked at me.**

This poem provides practice in the use of the *subject pronouns,* **I, he, we;** the *object pronouns,* **me, him, them;** and the *possessive adjective,* **his.**

Notice the use of *prepositions of place* followed by the *definite article:* **in the, on the, near the;** and the use of *prepositions in phrases:* **to look at, to be scared of, to play with.**

This poem introduces the use of **both** and **each other,** and illustrates the use of **hope** to express a wish for the future.

PRESENTATION:
See page ix for suggestions on presenting the poems.

NOTES

_____

_____

_____

_____

_____

_____

_____

_____

_____

_____

_____

ACTIVITY GUIDE

TASK:
Have the students draw a line from each vehicle on the left to the appropriate place for that vehicle on the right: either the road, the ocean, or the sky.

PRACTICE:
- 1. *Rhyming*
  Introduce the students to the concept of rhyming. Point out the fact that **Gus** and **bus** rhyme. Elicit from the students words that rhyme with **Gus** and **bus.** Then point out the fact that **Jane** and **train** rhyme. Elicit from the students words that rhyme with **Jane** and **train.** Point out the fact that **Mike** and **bike** rhyme. Elicit words that rhyme with **Mike** and **bike.** Continue this activity with other rhyming sounds.

- 2. *Prepositions*
  Practice the *preposition by* or *on* with various modes of transportation. Have the students repeat:

  He goes by train.
  She goes by plane.
  They go by car.
  They go by bike.
  We go on foot.
  You go on horseback.
  Gus goes by bus.

- 3. *Discussion*
  Have the students discuss the manner in which they go to school. Begin with the question, "How do you go to school?" and have them answer factually. For example: "I go by bus every day."

ENRICHMENT:
- 1. *Drawing*
  Have the students draw a picture of the vehicle they would most like to buy if they had all the money in the world.

- 2. *Drawing*
  Have the students draw a map indicating the route from their house to the school.

Gus Always Takes the Bus

16

NOTES

_____

_____

_____

_____

_____

_____

_____

_____

_____

_____

_____

_____

_____

_____

Gus Always Takes the Bus

Gus always takes the bus.
    Why?
Gus always takes the bus.
    Why?
    Why does he take the bus?
Because he loves it.
    He loves it.
Elaine always takes the plane.
    Why?
Elaine always takes the plane.
    Why?
    Why does she take the plane?
Because she likes it.
    She likes it.
Jane never takes the train.
    Why not?
Jane never takes the train.
    Why not?
    Why doesn't she take the train?
Because she hates it.
    She hates it.
Mike always rides his bike.
    Why?
Mike always rides his bike.
    Why?
    Why does he ride his bike?
Because he loves it.
    He loves it.

17

CHANT GUIDE

PRONUNCIATION:
Practice the pronunciation of **bus, plane, train, bike, it, not** and the contraction **doesn't.**

Listen to the sound of the third person s in **takes, loves, likes, hates** and **rides.**

Listen carefully to the intonation of the statement, **Gus always takes the bus,** and the question, **Why does he take the bus?**

Notice the intonation pattern of the short question forms: **Why? Why not?**

Notice the z sound in the pronunciation of **does, because, loves** and in the final s ending of **always.**

Notice the reduction in the sound of the words *does* and *he* as they occur in the question: **Why does he?**

STRUCTURE:
This chant provides practice in the *simple present tense statement* with emphasis on the use of the third person s.

Notice the use of the frequency words, **always** and **never.**

This chant illustrates the use of the *definite article* as it occurs in: **takes the bus; takes the plane; takes the train.**

It also illustrates the use of questions with: **Why does he . . . ? Why doesn't he . . . ?**

PRESENTATION:
The accompanying tape provides a model for the presentation of this chant.

NOTES

_____

_____

_____

_____

_____

_____

_____

_____

_____

_____

_____

_____

ACTIVITY GUIDE

TASK:
Have the students fill in the blanks under each column of the page, listing several activities that they do when the sun is shining, and several activities that they do when it's raining.

PRACTICE:
- 1. *Vocabulary*
  Introduce vocabulary for the weather:

  It's raining.
  It's cloudy.
  It's sunny.
  It's cold.
  It's hot.
  It's snowing.

- 2. *Discussion*
  Have the students read aloud the answers that they wrote on the Activity Page. Discuss the various things one can do when the sun is shining and when it's raining. Ask students how they feel about the weather.

ENRICHMENT:
- 1. Have the students draw a picture illustrating the weather during their favorite time of the year.

The Sun is Shining

What do you do when the sun is shining?	What do you do when it's raining?

I play outside.

I watch T.V.

18

NOTES

The Sun is Shining

The sun is shining.
I love the sun.
> Me too.

The sun is shining.
I love the sun.
> Me too.

The sun is shining.
I love the sun.
The sun is shining today.

It's raining today.
I love the rain.
> Not me.

It's raining today.
I love the rain.
> Not me.

It's raining today.
I love the rain.
It's raining, raining today.

It's snowing today.
I love the snow.
> I'm cold.

It's snowing today.
I love the snow.
> I'm cold.

It's snowing today.
I love the snow.
It's snowing, snowing today.

19

CHANT GUIDE

PRONUNCIATION:
Practice the pronunciation of **sun, love, today, not, cold** and **snow.** Practice the contractions: **I'm, it's.**

Listen carefully to the sound of the *-ing* ending in **shining, raining, snowing.**

STRUCTURE:
This song illustrates the contrast in the use of the *present continuous* and the *simple present tense.*

Notice that the *present continuous statement,* **The sun is shining,** refers to action occurring at this moment, temporary in nature, while the *simple present statement,* **I love the sun,** reflects an attitude, presumably permanent.

Notice that the use of the short forms, **me too** and **not me,** are acceptable in casual American English speech as substitutes for: I do too. / So do I.
I don't either. / Neither do I.

PRESENTATION:
Listen to the accompanying tape for the melody, tempo and style of presentation of this song.

NOTES

_____

_____

_____

_____

_____

_____

_____

_____

_____

_____

_____

_____

_____

_____

ACTIVITY GUIDE

TASK:
Using the example box as a model, have the students draw a line from the person or animal in the left column to what it is scared of in the right column.

PRACTICE:
- 1. *Subject Pronouns*
Present the basic sentence: **I'm scared of the dark.** Have the students repeat the sentence. Then substitute different subject pronouns in the subject position.

    T: I'm scared of the dark.
    T: She
    S: She's scared of the dark.
    T: He
    S: He's scared of the dark.
    T: You
    S: You're scared of the dark.

- 2. *Nouns*
Now, using the same sentence, substitute in the noun position.

    T: You're scared of the dark.
    T: Deep water.
    S: You're scared of deep water.
    T: Fire.
    S: You're scared of fire.
    T: Thunder.
    S: You're scared of thunder.

- 3. *Object Pronouns*
Now, using the same basic sentence, substitute for the object pronouns.

    T: You're scared of them.
    T: Her.
    S: You're scared of her.
    T: Me.
    S: You're scared of me.
    T: Him.
    S: You're scared of him.

- ● ● ● 4. *Subject Pronouns, Object Pronouns and Nouns*
For more advanced students, substitute within several slots at the same time.

    T: I'm scared of the dark.
    T: She . . . deep water.
    S: She's scared of deep water.
    T: He . . . her.
    S: He's scared of her.

ENRICHMENT:
- 1. Have the students draw a picture of the thing that is scariest to them.

- ● 2. *Discussion*
Discuss with the students what each one is most afraid of. Elicit from them what they do when they are scared.

Scaredy Cat

WHAT ARE THEY SCARED OF?

20

NOTES

_____

_____

_____

_____

_____

_____

_____

_____

_____

_____

_____

_____

_____

_____

Scaredy Cat

I'm afraid of the dark.
    Don't be silly.
I'm afraid of the dark.
    Don't be silly.
I'm scared of the dark.
    Don't be silly.
    Don't be silly.
I'm afraid of the dark.

Turn on the lights!
    Don't be silly.
Turn on the lights!
    Don't be silly.
Turn on the lights!
    Don't be silly.
Turn them on!
    Turn them off!

Turn them on!
    Turn them off!
Turn them on!
    Don't be silly.
    Don't be silly.
I'm afraid of the dark.

I'm scared of the dark.
    She's scared of the dark.
    Scaredy cat!
    Scaredy cat!
I'm scared of the dark.
    She's scared of the dark.
    Scaredy cat!
    Scaredy cat!
Turn on the lights!
    Don't be silly.
    Scaredy cat!
I'm afraid of the dark.

21

CHANT GUIDE

PRONUNCIATION:
Practice the pronunciation of the contractions: **I'm, don't, she's.**

Listen carefully to the pronunciation of **cat, dark, scared** and **silly.**

Notice the plural *s* in **lights** and the *th* sound in **them.**

STRUCTURE:
This chant provides practice in the *simple present tense statement* expressing fear: **I'm afraid of. . . . I'm scared of . . .**

Notice the use of the *command forms:* **Turn on the lights! Turn off the lights!**

PRESENTATION:
In presenting this chant, a variety of *subject pronouns* may be used in place of **she.** Refer to the ACTIVITY GUIDE, **Practice 1,** for a model substitution drill.

Notice that the expression, **Don't be silly,** is frequently used in response to a foolish statement. The expression, **Scaredy Cat,** is often used by children in the United States to tease a person who is easily frightened.

NOTES

_____
_____
_____
_____
_____
_____
_____
_____
_____
_____
_____
_____
_____

ACTIVITY GUIDE

TASK:

Have the students locate **Grandma's house, the movies, the dentist's office,** and **the doctor's office** on the map by either tracing the route to each of these with their fingers or by drawing each route with a different colored crayon.

PRACTICE:

- 1. *Questions Using the Past Tense*

    Have the students transform your statements into questions using the *past tense*.

    T: I turned at the corner.
    S: Where did you turn?
    T: I walked down the street.
    S: Where did you walk?
    T: I went to the store.
    S: Where did you go?
    (Teach this form as a separate vocabulary item to the students: *go / went*.)

- 2. *Vocabulary*

    Teach vocabulary for giving and following directions.

    Turn left.
    Turn right.
    Walk two blocks.
    Go straight ahead.

- 3. *Listen and Comprehension*

    Have the students each look at their map, studying the street names and the locations of different buildings carefully. You give directions, having them trace the route with their fingers. For example, you might say: "He walked up Main Street, turned right on Second Street, walked across Spring Street and stopped at the corner. Where is he?" The first student to answer, "At the grocery store," would be correct.

ENRICHMENT:

- 1. *Drawing*

    Have the students draw a map showing the route from their home to the school, indicating known landmarks along the way.

- 2. *Game*

    Have one student hide something, either within the bounds of the classroom or within the larger bounds of the school. Have that student give directions to the other students so that they may find where the object is hidden.

    For example: "Go down the stairs, turn right and walk to the end of the hall." The first child to find the object according to the directions is the winner and becomes the next leader.

Where's Jack?

WHERE'S JACK? WHERE DID HE GO?

Find:
Grandma's house.
The movies.
The dentist's office.
The doctor's office.

22

NOTES

_____
_____
_____
_____
_____
_____
_____
_____
_____
_____
_____
_____
_____
_____
_____

Where's Jack?

Where's Jack?
> He's not here.

Where did he go?
> I don't know.

Where's Mary?
> She's not here.

Where did she go?
> I don't know.

Where are Sue and Bobby?
> They're not here.

Where did they go?
> I don't know.

Where's Mr. Brown?
> He's over there.

Where?
> Over there,
> asleep in the chair.

23

CHANT GUIDE

PRONUNCIATION:
Practice the pronunciation of the contractions: **where's, he's, she's, don't, they're.**
Practice the pronunciation of **Mr., asleep, know, chair** and **over.**

Listen carefully to the pronunciation of **not, here** and to the *th* sound in **there** and **they're.**

Listen to the reduction in the sound of the word *did* when it occurs in the past tense question: **Where did he go?** Notice that the *h* sound in *he* is dropped in **did he.**

Notice the intonation pattern in the one-word question, **Where?**

Practice the intonation pattern of the question, **Where's Jack?** and the response statement, **He's not here.**

STRUCTURE:
This chant provides practice in the *simple present tense question,* **Where's Jack?** and the *negative response* statement, **He's not here.**

It also illustrates the frequently used combination of *simple past tense question,* **Where did he go?** answered by the *simple present tense statement,* **I don't know.**

Notice the use of the *subject pronouns:* **I, he, she, they.**

PRESENTATION:
The accompanying tape provides a model for the presentation of this chant.

NOTES

_____

_____

_____

_____

_____

_____

_____

_____

_____

_____

_____

_____

ACTIVITY GUIDE

TASK:
Using the example as a model, have the students write the answers for each picture, 1 to 4. The correct answers follow:

1. He ate it.
2. They tore it.
3. She wore it.
4. He lost it.

PRACTICE:
- 1. *Vocabulary*
  Teach the *irregular* past forms for the following verbs:

do / did	come / came
go / went	sing / sang
run / ran	lose / lost

- • 2. *What and Where Questions*
  Have the students transform statements into questions using the *past tense* of *irregular verbs* taught in **Practice 1** above. Notice that this exercise calls for the students to ask either *What questions* or *Where questions.*

  T: He ate it.
  S: What did he eat?
  T: He went home.
  S: Where did he go?
  T: She sang a song.
  S: What did she sing?
  T: She ran home.
  S: Where did she run?
  T: They came here.
  S: Where did they come?

ENRICHMENT:
- 1. *Game*
  Have the students gather in a circle, with one student in the center. Have the student leader in the center perform an action. Have each student in the circle imitate the action. Then ask the question, "What did he do?" The first student to answer using the correct past tense form of the verb becomes the new leader.

You Did It Again!

What did she do? She broke it.

1. What did he do?   2. What did they do?

3. What did she do?   4. What did he do?

24

NOTES

_____
_____
_____
_____
_____
_____
_____
_____
_____
_____
_____
_____
_____

You Did It Again!

You did it again!
　　　　What did I do?
You did it again!
　　　　What did I do?
I told you not to do it,
and you did it again!
　　　　I'm sorry.
　　　　I'm sorry.

You broke it!
　　　　What did I break?
You took it!
　　　　What did I take?
You lost it!
　　　　What did I lose?

You chose it!
　　　　What did I choose?
I told you not to do it,
and you did it again!
　　　　I'm sorry.
　　　　I'm sorry.

You wore it!
　　　　What did I wear?
You tore it!
　　　　What did I tear?
I told you not to do it,
and you did it again!
　　　　I'm sorry.
　　　　I'm sorry.

25

PRONUNCIATION:
Practice the pronunciation of: **it, again, break, broke, take, took, lose, lost, choose, chose, wear, wore, tear, tore, not.**
Practice the pronunciation of the contraction, **I'm.**

Listen to the reduction in the sound of *did* when it occurs in the question, **What did I do?** as contrasted to the full sound of *did* in the statement, **You did it again!**

Notice the strong expression of feeling in the intonation pattern of the accusing statement, **You did it again!** contrasted with the question response, **What did I do?** and the apologetic rejoinder, **I'm sorry.**
Notice that the degree of anger, confusion and apology is expressed through the *intonation* as well as the choice of words themselves.

STRUCTURE:
This chant provides practice in the *simple past tense statement* and *question* with special emphasis on the *irregular verb forms:* **do / did, break / broke, lose / lost, choose / chose, wear / wore, tear / tore.**

Notice the *indirect command pattern:* **I told you not to. . . .**

PRESENTATION:
This chant may be easily expanded to include practice in the *subject pronouns:* he, she, they, we; and a wide variety of *regular* and *irregular verbs.* Example: He found it. They burned it.

NOTES
_____
_____
_____
_____
_____
_____
_____
_____
_____
_____
_____
_____
_____

ACTIVITY GUIDE

TASK:
Have the students circle the hidden words in the picture and then write them in the spaces provided. The words in the fish are: **cat, birds, fly, we, baby, swim, he, bark, fish, cry.**

PRACTICE:
- 1. *Vocabulary*
    Introduce vocabulary for animal names and activities.

    Dogs: bark, growl
    Birds: fly
    Cats, Kittens: purr
    Fish: swim
    Insects: fly, crawl
    Horses: gallop, trot, run

- 2. *Questions with do and short answer responses*
    Using the vocabulary suggested above, and that which you have added to it, ask the students about each of the animals and have them answer factually, using the simple present tense and short answer response.

    T: Do dogs bark?
    S1: Yes, they do.
    T: Do dogs fly?
    S2: No, they don't.
    T: Do cats gallop?
    S3: No, they don't.

- 3. *Discussion*
    Discuss with the students what life was like when they were babies or simply when they were younger. Have each student tell one thing that he *used to do* when he was a baby. Be sure the students use the *habitual past tense* with *used to*.

ENRICHMENT:
- 1. *Drawing*
    Have the students draw a picture of the animal they would most like to be, if they could be an animal. If the students are advanced enough, ask them what that animal can do that a human being cannot, and what a human being can do that the animal cannot.

- 2. *Game*
    Have each student bring in an old baby picture. Put all the pictures on the bulletin board with the name of each student on the back of the photograph. Then have the children guess which picture belongs to which student.

When I Was a Baby

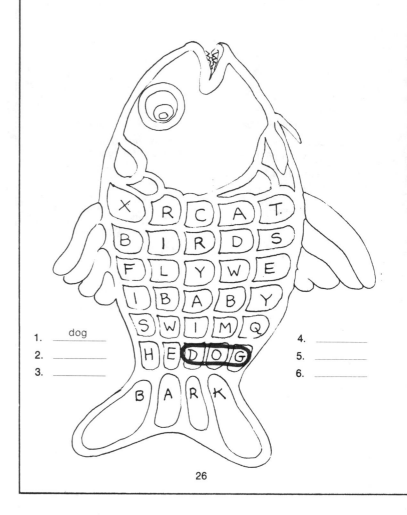

1. ___dog___
2. _____
3. _____
4. _____
5. _____
6. _____

26

NOTES

_____
_____
_____
_____
_____
_____
_____
_____
_____
_____
_____
_____

When I Was a Baby

When I was a baby, a baby, a baby,
When I was a baby, I used to cry.
When I was a baby, a baby, a baby,
When I was a baby, I used to cry.

When I was a dog, I used to bark.
When I was a kitten, I used to purr.
When I was a bird, I used to fly.
But when I was a baby, a baby, a baby,
When I was a baby, I used to cry.

When I was a fish, I used to swim.
When I was a tiger, I used to bite.
When I was a bluebird, I used to fly.
But when I was a baby, a baby, a baby,
When I was a baby, I used to cry.

27

CHANT GUIDE

PRONUNCIATION:
Practice the pronunciation of **when, baby, bark, kitten, purr, tiger, bluebird, swim.**

Listen to the final *sh* sound in **fish.**

Notice that the sound of *d* disappears in **used to.**

STRUCTURE:
This song provides practice in the *past tense time clause,* **When I was,** followed by the *habitual past tense,* **I used to,** to indicate a repeated action or condition in the past which is no longer true.

Notice the use of the word **but** to introduce an opposing idea.

PRESENTATION:
Listen to the accompanying tape for the melody, tempo and style of presentation of this song.

NOTES

_____
_____
_____
_____
_____
_____
_____
_____
_____
_____
_____
_____

ACTIVITY GUIDE

TASK:
Have the students complete the word puzzle, using the clues at the bottom of the page. For example: **Not the truth** is given as the clue for the first item across, **lie.** The complete puzzle will contain the words: **lie, in, short, truth, end, near.**

PRACTICE:
● 1. *Listen and Comprehension*
The first two lines of the chant may be used as the basis for an oral exercise in the *command forms,* followed by a *response* in the *present continuous.* Have the students use the *-ing* form of the same verb you do. Have the students actually perform the action the command calls for as they say the response.

T: Look at me.
S: I'm looking at you.
T: Stand up.
S: I'm standing up.
T: Sit down.
S: I'm sitting down.
T: Put your hands in your lap.
S: I'm putting my hands in my lap.

●● 2. *Vocabulary*
Using the picture activity as a point of departure, explain opposites. For example: A **lie** is the opposite of the **truth.** A suggested list of opposites follows:

tall / short	out / in
far / near	up / down
over / under	big / small
good / bad	same / different
begin / end	

●● 3. Have the students use each of the words in **Practice 2,** above, in a sentence.

ENRICHMENT:
●● 1. *Game*
Group the students in two teams, A and B. Have one member from Team A give commands to people on Team B and vice versa. Each team gives one command at a time, in turn. A command should involve doing physical activities that are somewhat difficult and fun. For example: ''Close your eyes, put your right heel on your left knee, and hold that position for fifteen seconds.''

●●● 2. *Puzzle*
Have the students make their own crossword puzzle. One way to do this is to have them write down all of the words they would like in the crossword puzzle, then have them write a definition for each word. They can easily do this by listing the definitions in terms of the opposites they practiced earlier

Listen To Me

1. Not the truth
2. Not out
3. Not tall
4. Not a lie
5. Not the beginning
6. Not far

28

NOTES

_____

_____

_____

_____

_____

_____

_____

_____

_____

_____

_____

_____

Listen To Me

Listen to me.
> I'm listening.

Listen to me.
> I'm listening.

Listen to me.
> I am, I am.

Answer me.
> I will, I will.

Answer me.
> I will, I will.

Tell me the truth.
> I will, I will.

Tell me the truth.
> I will, I will.

Don't tell a lie.
> I won't, I won't.

Don't tell a lie.
> I won't, I won't.

Tell me the truth.
> I will.

Answer me.
> I will.

Listen to me.
> I am.

29

CHANT GUIDE

PRONUNCIATION:
Practice the pronunciation of the contractions: **I'm, won't, don't.**
Practice the pronunciation of **listen** and **answer.**

Listen to the *-ing* sound in **listening** and the *th* sound in **truth.**

Notice the difference in the sound of the contraction **I'm** and the short emphatic response, **I am.**

STRUCTURE:
This chant provides practice in the *command forms:* **listen, answer, tell, don't tell;** followed by a response either in the *present continuous,* **I'm listening;** or the short response, **I will / I won't,** to indicate a promise.

Notice the use of the *definite* and *indefinite articles* as they occur in **a lie, the truth;** and the *preposition to* as it occurs in **listen to.**

PRESENTATION:
The accompanying tape provides a model for the presentation of this chant.

NOTES

ACTIVITY GUIDE

TASK:
Have the students complete the maze, starting with the arrow marked **Start,** continuing through the appropriate areas to the final goal of the **Lemonade.**

PRACTICE:

•• 1. *Direct and Indirect Objects*
Have the students practice with *indirect* and *direct objects* by having them substitute within the sentence: **I asked my mother for a candy bar.** You provide the cues for substitution.

T: I asked my <u>mother</u> for <u>a candy bar.</u>
T: father . . . fifty cents.
S: I asked my father for fifty cents.
T: teacher . . . a cookie.
S: I asked my teacher for a cookie.
T: friend . . . some ice cream.
S: I asked my friend for some ice cream.

••• 2. *Discussion*
Have each student tell about one thing they asked someone for. Have the other students ask, "What did he/she say?"

ENRICHMENT:

• 1. *Role Play*
Have students work in groups of two and role play the act of asking someone for something. Some typical situations might include: parent / child, teacher / student, brother / sister. Let the students decide what they will ask for and whether or not they will grant the request.

The role play could be expanded, depending upon the language level of the students. For example: If Student 1 asks for something and Student 2 says, "No," then Student 1 could pursue the conversation by asking, "Why not?" Student 2 would then have to provide a reasonable answer.

I Asked My Father

30

NOTES

_____

_____

_____

_____

_____

_____

_____

_____

_____

_____

_____

_____

_____

_____

I Asked My Father

I asked my father.
               What did he say?
Papa said, "No, no, no."

I asked my mother.
               What did she say?
Mama said, "Yes, yes, yes."

I asked my father for a dollar and a half.
               What did he say?
No, no.

I asked my mother for fifty cents.
               What did she say?
No, no.

I asked Mom again.
               What did she say?
My mother said, "Ask your father."

I asked Dad again.
               What did he say?
My father said, "Ask your mother."

I asked my mother for a candy bar.
               What did she say?
No, no.

I asked my father for some lemonade.
               What did he say?
Yes, yes.

31

CHANT GUIDE

PRONUNCIATION:
Listen carefully to the pronunciation of **asked, bar, say, said, fifty, again.**
Listen to the sound of the plural *s* in **cents.**

Notice the *t* sound in the past tense ending of the word **asked,** the *th* sound in **mother, father** and the *sh* sound in **she.**
Notice that the sound of the letter *h* is often dropped when it occurs in **did he** and **asked him.**

Listen to the reduction in the sound of the word *did* when it occurs in the question: **What did he say?**

Practice the intonation pattern of the statement, **I asked my mother,** and the question, **What did she say?**

STRUCTURE:
This chant provides practice in the *simple past tense statement* followed by a *question:* **I asked my mother. What did she say?**

It illustrates the use of the *subject pronouns,* **I, she, he;** the *object pronoun,* **him;** and the *possessive adjectives,* **my, your.**

Notice the use of the *preposition for* as it occurs in the pattern to *ask someone for something:* I asked my father **for** some lemonade.

This chant also provides examples of reported speech: **My father said, "Ask your mother."**

PRESENTATION:
The accompanying tape provides a model for the presentation of this chant.

NOTES

ACTIVITY GUIDE

TASK:

Have the students connect the dots. Have them begin by drawing a line from number **1** to number **2** and so forth through number **81**. Then, have them connect the dots between the letters, beginning with letter **A**, continuing to letter **B** and so forth through letter **P**. The completed picture will reveal a cat sitting on a hat.

The second part of the **TASK** is for the students to circle as many words as they can find in the sleeping cat at the bottom of the page. Have them write the words in the spaces provided. The following words appear in the body of the cat: **cat, art, hen, of, hat, my, on, sat, fat, the, new, me, then.**

Have the students arrange the words they have found to reveal the secret message: **The fat cat sat on my hat.**

PRACTICE:

1. Review numbers and letters for students who still have trouble with them.

● 2. *Present tense with have got.*
    Have the students practice using *have got* in place of *have* to indicate possession. Point out that the contractions, *he's, she's,* as they occur in **he's got** and **she's got** represent *he+has+got* and *she+has+got*, rather than *he* or *she + is.*

    Have the students repeat the model sentence: **I've got a secret.** Then have them substitute subject pronouns after you provide the cue.

    T: I've got a secret.
    T: She
    S: She's got a secret.
    T: He
    S: He's got a secret.
    T: They
    S: They've got a secret.
    T: We
    S: We've got a secret.
    T: You
    S: You've got a secret.

ENRICHMENT:

● 1. *Game: Telephone*
    Begin by whispering a secret sentence to the first student. That student then whispers the same sentence to the next student and so forth, around the room, until the last student repeats the secret sentence aloud. Compare the final result with the initial sentence.

●● 2. *Game*
    Have three or four different students whisper a secret to you. Write each secret in scrambled word order on the board. Have students unscramble (either orally or on paper) each secret sentence.

sat _____

32

NOTES

_____
_____
_____
_____
_____
_____
_____
_____
_____
_____
_____
_____
_____
_____

I've Got a Secret

I've got a secret, I won't tell.
I've got a secret, I won't tell.
I've got a secret, I won't tell.
I won't tell anybody here.
  Tell me, tell me.

I won't tell.
  Tell me, tell me.

I won't tell.
  Tell me, tell me.

I won't tell.
I won't tell anybody here.
  Say it softly.

I won't say it.
  Say it softly.

I won't say it.
  Say it softly.

I won't say it.
  Whisper it in my ear.
  Tell me, tell me.

I won't tell you.
  Tell him, tell him.

I won't tell him.
  Tell her, tell her.

I won't tell her.
I won't tell anybody here.
  Whisper it softly. *pss pss*
  Whisper it softly. *pss pss*
  Whisper it softly. *pss pss*
  I won't tell anybody here.

I'll whisper it to you. *pss pss*
I'll whisper it to you. *pss pss*
I'll whisper it to you, *pss pss*
but don't tell anybody here.
  I won't!

33

PRONUNCIATION:
Practice the pronunciation of the contractions: **I've, won't, I'll, don't.**

Listen carefully to the pronunciation of the words **secret, it, softly, whisper.**

Notice that the sound of the *h* in *her* and *him* disappears when it occurs in **tell her, tell him.**

STRUCTURE:
This song provides practice in the *simple present tense statement* using *have got,* in place of *have,* to indicate possession, as in **I've got a secret.**

Notice the use of *won't* to express *refusal,* as in **I've got a secret, I won't tell;** or to indicate a *promise,* as in the final short response, **I won't.**

The song illustrates the use of the affirmative and negative *command forms:* **tell, don't tell;** and the *object pronouns:* **me, her, him, it.**

PRESENTATION:
This song is based on the traditional folk melody, "Skip to My Lou." Listen to the tape for the melody, tempo and style of presentation of this song.

NOTES

ACTIVITY GUIDE

TASK:

Have the students look at the example box. Then, have them complete the sentences under each picture, using the correct object pronoun: **her, him, it, them.** The answers are as follows:

1. He's mad at **her.**
2. She's mad at **him.**
3. They're mad at **them.**
4. He's mad at **her.**
5. He's mad at **it.**
6. She's mad at **them.**

PRACTICE:

● 1. *Object Pronouns*

Give the students a sentence using the name or names of students in the class. Have the students answer individually or chorally by substituting the appropriate object pronoun for the student or students you named.

T: I like Farrah.
S: I like her.
T: She's mad at Raul.
S: She's mad at him.
T: Amy gave Noriko and Lee cookies.
S: Amy gave them cookies.

●● 2. *Subject and Object Pronouns*

Continue **Practice 1** above, this time, however, use student names in both subject and object positions in the sentence and have the class substitute the correct subject and object pronouns.

T: John's mad at Susan.
S: He's mad at her.
T: Debra likes Donna and Luis.
S: She likes them.

●●● 3. *Discussion*

Have students tell what makes them angry and what they do when they're angry. Explain that in different cultures people react to anger differently.

ENRICHMENT:

● 1. *Drawing*

Have the students draw a picture of what they think they look like when they are angry.

●● 2. *Role Play*

Have two students act out a situation where one person says or does something to make the other person angry. The angry person responds verbally, using the model: **I'm mad at you.** The role play will vary tremendously from group to group depending on the age, sophistication and language level of the students involved.

If appropriate, you may wish to introduce a discussion of acceptable and unacceptable ways to express verbal anger in polite company.

I'm Mad at You

1. He's mad at _her_
2. She's mad at _____.
3. They're mad at _____.
4. He's mad at _____.
5. He's mad at _____.
6. She's mad at _____.

34

NOTES

34

I'm Mad at You

I'm mad at you.
        What did I do?
I'm mad at you.
        What did I do?
I'm mad at you.
        What did I do?
        What's the matter?
I'm mad at you.

I'm mad at her.
        What did she do?
I'm mad at her.
        What did she do?
I'm mad at her.
        What did she do?
        What's the matter?
I'm mad at you.

I'm mad at him.
        What did he do?
I'm mad at him.
        What did he do?
I'm mad at him.
        What did he do?
        What's the matter?
I'm mad at you.

35

CHANT GUIDE

PRONUNCIATION:
Practice the pronunciation of the contractions: **I'm, what's.**

Notice the reduction in the sound of the word *did* when it occurs in the question: **What did I do?**

Listen carefully to the contrast in the intonation patterns of the statement, **I'm mad at you,** and the question response, **What did I do?**
Listen carefully to the pronunciation of **mad** and **matter.**

STRUCTURE:
This chant provides practice in the *simple present tense statement,* **I'm mad at you,** followed by the simple past tense question, **What did I do?**

It also illustrates the high frequency combination of *simple past* and *simple present tense questions:* **What did I do? What's the matter?**

Notice the use of the *subject pronouns,* **I, he, she**; and the *object pronouns,* **you, her, him.**
Notice the use of the *preposition at* as it occurs in the expression, **mad at.**

PRESENTATION:
The accompanying tape provides a model for the presentation of this chant.

NOTES

ACTIVITY GUIDE

TASK:
Have the students complete the picture poem by filling in the appropriate word, either orally or in writing, in the blank space above each picture. The picture poem should read: My **cat** loves to sleep on my **bed.** His **feet** are often **dirty.** Sometimes he takes a nap on my **lap,** And he sleeps 'till **7:30.**

PRACTICE:
- 1. *Vocabulary*
  Introduce vocabulary for the students to substitute in the blank spaces in the picture poem, in order to create a new poem. For example: My *dog / bird / hamster* loves to *walk / dance / jump* on my *bed / table / rug,* etc.

- ● 2. Following the model of the **Four Short Poems,** have students write or say their own poems. Suggest the topics and suggest that they keep it to four lines, which hopefully rhyme. Have the students write one poem about something they love and one poem about something they don't like.

ENRICHMENT:
- 1. *Drawing*
  Have the students draw a picture of something they like and something they don't like to go with the poems they have written or said aloud.

- ● 2. *Picture Poem*
  Have the students create their own picture poems by drawing pictures in certain spaces in a sentence and leaving a blank space above the pictures as is indicated in the model picture poem on page 36. When the poems are complete, have the students exchange papers and fill in the blanks on the poem that their neighbor wrote.

Four Short Poems

MY FAT CAT

My ___cat___ loves to _____ on my _____.

His _____ are often _____.

Sometimes he takes a nap on my _____,

and he sleeps 'till_____.

36

NOTES

_____

_____

_____

_____

_____

_____

_____

_____

_____

_____

_____

_____

_____

Four Short Poems

My Brother Broke Our TV Set

My brother broke our TV set.
My sister cracked a dish.
My father wrecked our brand-new car.
Our housecat ate my fish.

I Hate The Dentist

I love coffee.
I love tea.
I hate the dentist
and the dentist hates me.

Mice Are Nice

I think mice
are very nice.
Mice are nice.
Mice are furry.
Mice are often
in a hurry.
I don't really want to be one,
but I'm happy when I see one.

Cats Love to Sleep

Cats love to sleep in the sunshine.
Cats love to sleep in the shade.
But my cat sleeps in the middle of my bed,
on the blankets,
when the bed's not made.

37

NOTES

_____

_____

_____

_____

CHANT GUIDE

PRONUNCIATION:
Practice the pronunciation of **brother, sister, father,** and **dentist.** Practice the pronunciation of **very, furry, hurry, happy** and **often.**

Listen for the third person *s* in **hates** and **loves.**

Practice the initial *th* sound in **think,** the *sh* sound in **sunshine, fish, dish, shade,** and the *t* sound of the past tense ending in **cracked** and **wrecked.**

Notice the *s* sound in the ending of **mice** and **nice.** Practice the contractions: **I'm, don't.**

STRUCTURE:
My Brother Broke Our TV Set offers practice in the *regular* and *irregular past tense* verb forms: **cracked, wrecked, broke** and **ate;** and illustrates the use of the *possessive adjectives,* **my** and **our.**

I Hate the Dentist is written in the *simple present tense.* This poem includes an illustration of the third person *s* in **hates,** and the use of the *subject* and *object pronouns,* **I** and **me.**

Mice Are Nice presents the *simple present tense* in affirmative and negative statements. Notice the use of the *irregular plural* form **mice,** the frequency word **often,** and the use of the subject pronoun **one** as it occurs in the sentence, **I don't want to be one.** This poem includes a *time clause* with *when* as it occurs in, **when I see one.**
Notice the use of *really* for emphasis in the phrase: **I don't really want to. . . .**

Cats Love to Sleep illustrates the *simple present tense,* third person singular, **my cat sleeps,** and the third person plural, **cats love to sleep.**
Notice the use of the *prepositions in* and *on,* and the *definite article the* as they occur in the expressions: **in the sunshine; in the shade; in the middle; on the blankets.**

PRESENTATION:
See page ix for suggestions on presenting the poems.

ACTIVITY GUIDE

TASK:

Have the students answer the questions by locating each item (bicycle, briefcase, umbrella and books) in the appropriate closet. The correct answers are:

1. It's in Mary's closet.
2. It's in Mr. Murphy's closet.
3. It's in Mrs. Murphy's closet.
4. They're in Bill's closet.

PRACTICE:

● 1. *Where Questions*

Use the picture of the **Murphy's closets** as the basis for further practice with *Where questions.* Use both singular and plural forms in real question and answer practice and have students actually locate each item.

T: Where's the guitar?
S: It's in Bill Murphy's closet.
T: Where are the dresses?
S: They're in Mrs. Murphy's closet.

●● 2. *What Questions*

Have the students practice vocabulary for the items in each closet. Then, have them produce these words as answers to *What questions.*

T: What's in Mrs. Murphy's closet?
S: There are shoes, dresses, an umbrella, a box, blankets, etc.

●●● 3. *Discussion*

Have students tell about some of the things they have in their own closets.

ENRICHMENT:

● 1. *Game*

Collect several objects that are easily identifiable as belonging to particular children in the class. Choose one student to be *It* and select one of the objects. That student then asks questions such as, ''Is this John's?'' ''Is this Mary's?'' (Substitute the real names of children in the class.) Other students answer truthfully, ''Yes, it is.'' or ''No, it isn't.'' The person who identifies the correct owner of the object becomes *It,* and the game is begun again using another object.

Where's Mine? Is This Mine?

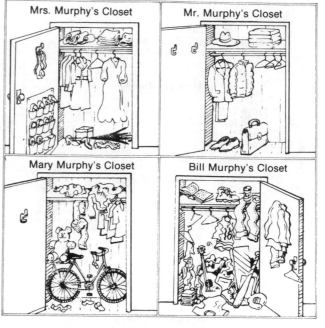

Where's the baseball bat? It's in Bill's closet.

1. Where's the bicycle? _____
2. Where's the briefcase? _____
3. Where's the umbrella? _____
4. Where are the books? _____

38

NOTES

_____
_____
_____
_____
_____
_____
_____
_____
_____
_____
_____
_____
_____
_____

Where's Mine? Is This Mine?

Where's mine? Is this mine?

No, that's hers.

Where's mine? Is this mine?

No, that's his.

Where are mine? Are these mine?

No, those are theirs.

Where are mine? Where are mine?

Yours are there,
on the chair.

Where?

On the chair.

39

PRONUNCIATION:
This chant illustrates the *contrasting* intonation patterns of the *information question,* **Where's mine?** and the *yes / no question,* **Is this mine?**

Practice the pronunciation of the contractions: **where's, that's.**
Practice the pronunciation of **this, that, these,** and **those.**

Listen to the *z* sound of the final *s* in **hers, yours,** and **theirs.**

Notice the long, stretched out sound of **mine.**
Notice the reduction in the sound of the word *are* when it occurs in the question, **Where are mine?** and in the statement, **Those are theirs.**

STRUCTURE:
This chant provides practice in the *simple present tense information questions:* **Where is . . . ? Where are . . . ?**; and the *yes / no questions:* **Is this . . . ? Are these . . . ?**

It illustrates the use of the *possessive pronouns:* **mine, yours, his, hers, theirs;** and the *demonstratives:* **this, that, these, those.**

PRESENTATION:
The accompanying tape provides a model for the presentation of this chant.

NOTES

ACTIVITY GUIDE

TASK:
Have the students say or write the appropriate word in the space above each picture in the poems. The completed poems should read:

The **sun** is hot.
The **moon** is cold.
The **snow** is white.
The **stars** are old.

 Can you feel the wind?
 Can you touch the **stars?**
 Can you see their lovely light?
 Can you see the **moon** in the afternoon?
 Can you touch the **stars** at night?

PRACTICE:
- 1. Have the students read or repeat the poem aloud. See page ix for suggestions on presenting the poems.

- 2. Have the students give examples of other things which are *hot / cold / white / old*. For example: Summer is hot. Winter is cold. My paper is white. My dog is old. Then, have each student make up his own poem, using the four example words.

ENRICHMENT:
- 1. *Drawing*
 Have the students illustrate the poems that they wrote.

- 2. *Picture Poem*
 Have the students make up entirely new poems describing their favorite thing(s). They should use the picture poem format (as indicated on the Activity Page), illustrating one word in each sentence, and leaving a blank space above the picture. When the poems are completed, have students exchange papers with each other. Each student then fills in the words on his neighbor's poem.

What Color is the Sun?

The <u>sun</u> is hot.

The _____ is cold.

The _____ is white.

The _____ are old.

Can you feel the wind?

Can you touch the _____?

Can you see their lovely light?

Can you see the _____ in the afternoon?

Can you touch the _____ at night?

40

NOTES

_____
_____
_____
_____
_____
_____
_____
_____
_____
_____
_____
_____
_____
_____

What Color is the Sun?

What color is the sun?
> The sun is gold.

How does it feel?
> Nice and warm.

What color is the snow?
> The snow is white.

How does it feel?
> Nice and cold.

The sun feels good.
> How does it feel?

The sun feels good.
> How does it feel?

The sun is warm.
The sun is gold.
> The snow is white.
> The snow is cold.

The sun feels good.
> How does it feel?

The sun feels good.
> How does it feel?

The sun feels warm.
The snow feels cold.
> The snow is white.
> The sun is gold.

41

CHANT GUIDE

PRONUNCIATION:
Listen carefully to the pronunciation of **nice, warm, snow,** and **white.**

Listen for the *z* sound of the third person *s* in **feels.**

Notice the long, stretched out sound of **feel, gold** and **cold.**

Notice the reduction in the sound of *does* when it occurs in the question, **How does it feel?** and the reduction in the sound of *and* in **nice and cold.**

STRUCTURE:
This chant provides practice in *simple present tense questions* with **What** and **How.**

It also illustrates the use of the *simple present third person s* as it occurs in: **The sun feels good.**

Notice the use of the *simple present statement* with the verb *to be* as it occurs in: **The sun is gold. The snow is white.**

PRESENTATION:
The accompanying tape provides a model for the presentation of this chant.

NOTES

ACTIVITY GUIDE

TASK:
Have the students look at the picture and mark all illustrations of good manners with a star, and all illustrations of bad manners with an X. One example of each is marked in the picture.

PRACTICE:
Explain, in the simplest way possible, that people in other cultures sometimes consider different things polite or rude. In some countries, for example, it is extremely rude to point. In other countries, it is considered rude to express anger.

The picture illustrates what is considered polite in American culture. (The two girls on the left sitting up straight and eating or drinking quietly, and the two boys on the right doing the same.)

It also illustrates what is considered rude. (The boy sticking his fingers in the pie; the girl playing with her spaghetti; the boy who spilled his milk and is crouching on the bench; the cat and dog at the table; the girl eating spaghetti using her hands.)

● ● 1. Using the picture as a basis for an oral or written exercise, have the students describe what is happening in the picture, specifically pointing out what is considered polite or rude. For example: The girl is sitting up straight. The boy is putting his thumb in the pie.

● ● 2. *Discussion*
Have students discuss what they and their family consider polite and rude behavior in the following circumstances:

At the dinner table.
At church.
In the classroom.
In the playground, park, or schoolyard.

ENRICHMENT:
● 1. *Drawing*
Have the students draw pictures illustrating polite and rude behavior in any one of the situations listed under *Discussion.*

● ● 2. *Role Play*
Have students role play polite and rude behavior.

● ● 3. *Discussion and Role Play*
Have the students discuss and then role play polite and rude behavior for the situations listed below. Attempt to have the more sophisticated children role play verbal forms of politeness and rudeness.

Meeting someone for the first time.
Four students in a group. One has no lunch.
Two team captains are selecting players. There are two students left. One is an excellent player and the other is a poor player, but eager to participate.

The Elbows Song

42

NOTES

_____

_____

_____

_____

_____

_____

_____

_____

_____

_____

_____

_____

_____

The Elbows Song

Take your elbows
off the table.
Keep those big feet
on the floor.

Take your hat off
when you come in.
You're not outside,
anymore.

Keep your mouth shut
when you're eating.
If you're hungry,
ask for more.

But take your elbows
off the table,
and keep those big feet
on the floor.

43

CHANT GUIDE

PRONUNCIATION:
Practice the pronunciation of **take, off, keep, big, feet, floor, hat, not, ask** and **hungry.**

Listen to the pronunciation of the initial *th* sound in **those** and the final *th* sound in **mouth.**

Notice the *z* sound in the plural *s* ending of **elbows.** Practice the sound of the contraction **you're.**

STRUCTURE:
This song illustrates the *command forms* with the verbs **take, keep** and **ask.** It also introduces *time clauses* with *when* in the *simple present tense,* **when you come in,** and the *present continuous,* **when you're eating.**

Notice the use of the *prepositions* as they occur in the two-word verbs: **take off, keep on, ask for** and **come in.**

This song includes examples of *regular* and *irregular plurals,* **elbows, feet;** and the use of the *real conditional tense* followed by a *command form,* **If you're hungry, ask for more.** This pattern is frequently found in conversational American English.

PRESENTATION:
Listen to the accompanying tape for the melody, tempo and style of presentation of this song.

NOTES

ACTIVITY GUIDE

TASK:
Have the students locate the **Start Here** sign and follow the correct path in the maze until they reach the finish point and find the **Cow.**

PRACTICE:

- 1. *Vocabulary*
  Ask the students to name the other animals that they saw in the maze: elephant, dog, hen, rooster, pig, cat, mouse, bird, bear, snake, bee, squirrel, duck and cow. Practice this vocabulary if the students don't already know it.

- 2. Sounds associated with animals vary considerably in different countries (and languages). Teach the sounds typically associated, in American culture, with each animal in the picture. Have students tell what sounds each animal makes in their country (or native language). For example: In the United States (or in English), a cat says *Meow.* In _____ a cat says _____ .

- 3. *Past Tense Question with did*
  Practice a drill using the *past tense* and *question* with *did* to identify animals with their sounds. You introduce it, then have student-to-student practice.

    T: I found a *moo.*
    S1: What did she find?
    S2: She found a cow.
    S3: I heard a quack.
    S4: What did he hear?
    S5: He heard a duck.

ENRICHMENT:

- 1. *Role Play*
  Have each student pretend to be a particular animal performing the sound and actions associated with that animal. Have the other students guess which animal is being portrayed.

- 2. *Discussion*
  Have students discuss how they feel about one particular animal. They may have a favorite. If possible, discuss cultural values regarding the worth or worship of particular animals.

I Found a Cow

Find the cow.

44

NOTES

_____
_____
_____
_____
_____
_____
_____
_____
_____
_____
_____
_____
_____
_____
_____

When I Was One

When I was one
it wasn't much fun.

    What did you do
    when you were two?

When I was two
I learned to ski.

    What did you do
    when you were three?

When I was three
it was a bore.

    What did you do
    when you were four?

When I was four
I learned to drive.

    What did you do
    when you were five?

When I was five
I played with sticks.

    What did you do
    when you were six?

When I was six
it was really heaven.

    What did you do
    when you were seven?

When I was seven
I learned to skate.

    What did you do
    when you were eight?

When I was eight
it was really great,
but when I was one
it wasn't much fun.

49

CHANT GUIDE

PRONUNCIATION:
Practice the pronunciation of **three, ski, learned, played, really, skate** and **great.**
Practice the pronunciation of the numbers, **one** through **ten.**

Listen to the *z* sound of the *s* in **was, wasn't;** the final *th* sound in **with;** and the plural *s* in **sticks.**

Notice that the final *ed* in **learned** and **played** is pronounced with simply a *d* sound.
Notice the reduction in the sound of *did you* when it occurs in the question: **What did you do?**

STRUCTURE:
This chant illustrates the use of the *simple past tense* of the *regular verbs,* **learned, played;** and the *irregular verb be:* **was, were** and **wasn't.**

This chant provides repeated examples of the introductory *past tense time clause* with *when:* **When I was one.**
It also illustrates the verb plus infinitive pattern in: **I learned to drive.**

The chant provides words and expressions for vocabulary development such as: **to be fun, to be a bore.**

Note the use of *much* for emphasis in a negative statement: **It wasn't much fun.** The word *really* is used for emphasis in the affirmative statements: **It was really great. It was really heaven.**

PRESENTATION:
The accompanying tape provides a model for the presentation of this chant.

NOTES

ACTIVITY GUIDE

TASK:
Following the example, have the students draw a line connecting each matching pair of socks between the two clotheslines.

PRACTICE:
- 1. *Vocabulary*
  Using the picture as a reference, introduce vocabulary for comparisons and contrasts. Example:

  This sock is <u>bigger</u> than that one.
  > smaller
  > prettier
  > uglier
  > darker
  > lighter

  This sock is the <u>same</u> as that one.
  This sock is <u>different</u> from that one.
  This sock is the <u>best</u>.
  > worst
  > biggest
  > smallest

- 2. Using the vocabulary and patterns introduced in **Practice 1** above, expand the scope by describing other objects. Have several samples (two or more) of the same item. (For example, three pieces of chalk, two pencils, four books, three coins, etc.) Have the students describe them in relation to one another.

  T: (Holds up two pencils.)
  S: This pencil is bigger than that one.
  T: (Holds up three pencils.)
  S: This pencil is the biggest.
  T: (Holds up one book and two pencils.)
  S: The book is bigger than the pencils.

- 3. *Discussion*
  Have students break up into small conversation groups. Present two contrasting items to each group and have them discuss the similarities and differences and tell which one they prefer and why. The items may be either very simple, such as an apple and a chocolate candy bar, or they may elicit more complex comparisons such as a picture of a winter scene versus a summer scene, each with several activities going on. The actual items for comparison would depend on the age, language level, and interest level of the students.

ENRICHMENT:
- 1. *Game: One is Different*
  The object of this game is for students to select one item out of four that is different. The objects may be named orally by the teacher or a student, or they may be named and drawn on the board. The teacher asks, "Which one is different?", and then names four objects of which one is different.

Mama! Mama! My Socks Don't Match!

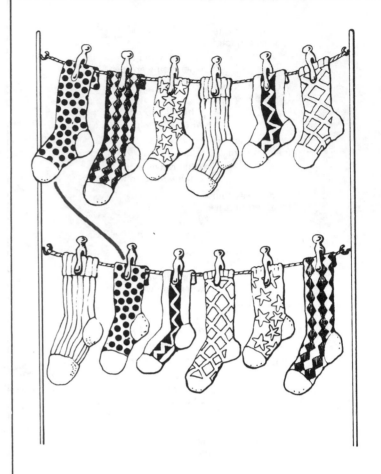

50

T: Which one is different?
Car, bus, train, shoe
S: Shoe
T: Boy, bird, girl, man
S: Bird
T: Chalk, pen, stick, pencil
S: Stick
T: Bear, nest, house, cage
S: Bear

Once the students understand the principle of the game, they can take the role of the teacher above and make up four items, one of which is different. The more advanced students can discuss why one item in a list is not part of that category.

Mama! Mama!
My Socks Don't Match!

Mama! Mama! My socks don't match!
One is red and one is blue.
One is bigger than the other!

                  Oh, no!

Mama! Mama! My socks don't match!
One is bigger than the other!

                  Oh, no!

Mama! Mama! My shoes don't match!
One is black and one is brown.
One is bigger than the other!

                  Oh, no!

Mama! Mama! My feet don't match!
One is bigger than the other!

                  Oh, no!

51

CHANT GUIDE

PRONUNCIATION:
Practice the *sh* sound in **shoes** and the *ch* sound in **match.** Practice the pronunciation of **blue, black, other** and the contraction **don't.**

Notice the *s* sound of the plural *s* in **socks** and the *z* sound of the plural *s* in **shoes.**

STRUCTURE:
This chant provides practice in *simple present tense statements,* both affirmative and negative.

It illustrates the use of the *comparative form,* **bigger than.** It also provides practice in the colors **red, blue, black** and **brown.**

Notice the *irregular plural* form **feet** and the use of **one** and **the other.**

PRESENTATION:
The accompanying tape provides a model for the presentation of this chant.

NOTES

ACTIVITY GUIDE

TASK:

Using the example as a model, have the students look at each picture and write or say a sentence describing the activity in each picture. Be sure the students use the *subject pronoun* with the *present continuous form* of the verb for each picture. The answers follow:

1. He's laughing.
2. They're running.
3. She's knocking (at the door).
4. They're crying.
5. He's whistling (or singing).
6. They're fighting.

PRACTICE:

● 1. *Vocabulary*

Review the vocabulary from the chant which describes the various sounds people make: **laughing, singing, crying, giggling, knocking.** Introduce related vocabulary which further describes various sounds people can make: whistling, yawning, snoring, scratching, tapping, coughing, sneezing, humming, choking, and wheezing. Either demonstrate or have students demonstrate the meaning of these words. Have the students repeat them in sentences after you. For example: "He's yawning" or "_____(student's name) is yawning."

●● 2. *Discussion*

Using the picture activity as a reference, ask the students to discuss the probable reason why the person (or the people) in each picture is doing what he's doing. For example, you might ask for **Number 1,** "Why is he laughing?" For **Number 2,** "Why are they running?"

Students should be encouraged to express their own imaginative ideas in answering the questions. Explain that there is no right answer and the answer depends on what they imagine.

ENRICHMENT:

● 1. *Role Play*

Have individual students pantomime an activity, such as somebody crying, knocking, laughing, etc. Have the students make no sounds while they are pantomiming the action. Have the student audience describe what that person is doing. For example: "He's crying." "He's knocking on his desk." "She's laughing."

●● 2. *Drawing*

Have the students draw a picture of a person performing one of the activities discussed in class, such as singing, laughing, crying, etc. Have them label the picture telling what the person in the picture is doing, and why that person is doing it.

Who's Knocking at the Door?

WHAT ARE THEY DOING?

She's singing.

1. _____
2. _____
3. _____
4. _____
5. _____
6. _____

52

NOTES

_____
_____
_____
_____
_____
_____
_____
_____
_____
_____
_____
_____
_____
_____
_____

Who's Knocking at the Door?

Listen!
    What?
Somebody's singing.
I hear somebody singing.
          La, la, la, la, la.
Listen!
    What?
Somebody's laughing.
I hear somebody laughing.
          Ha, ha, ha, ha, ha.
Listen!
    What?
Somebody's giggling.
I hear somebody giggling.
          Hee, hee, hee, hee.
Listen!
    What?
Somebody's crying.
I hear somebody crying.
          Boo-hoo, boo-hoo.
Listen!
    What?

I hear somebody knocking.
Somebody's knocking at the door.
          Knock, knock.
Who's singing?
    She is.
Who's laughing?
    He is.
Who's giggling?
    I am.
Who's crying?
    They are.
I wonder who's knocking
at the door?
          Knock, knock.
    Who's there?
          Knock, knock.
    Who's there?
          Knock, knock.
    Who's there?
I wonder who's knocking
at the door?

53

CHANT GUIDE

PRONUNCIATION:
Practice the pronunciation of **who, they, there, knock, door** and **wonder**.
Practice pronouncing the contrasting sounds of **they** and **there**.

Listen to the *-ing* sound in the ending of **singing, laughing, giggling, crying** and **knocking**.

Listen carefully to the intonation patterns of the command, **Listen;** the one-word question, **What?;** and the statement response, **Somebody's singing.**

STRUCTURE:
This chant provides practice in the *present continuous tense statement and question:* **Somebody's singing. Who's singing?**
It illustrates the *simple present tense statement,* **I hear somebody . . . ,** and *question,* **Who's there?**

The chant also illustrates the use of the *subject pronouns:* **I, she, he, they.**

Notice the use of **somebody** and the *preposition at* as it occurs in the expression **at the door.**

PRESENTATION:
The accompanying tape provides a model for the presentation of this chant.

NOTES
_____
_____
_____
_____
_____
_____
_____
_____
_____
_____
_____
_____

ACTIVITY GUIDE

TASK:

Have the students look at the example, while you pronounce the word **Boat.** Have the students spell it, and then have them pronounce it. Following the example, have the students identify each picture, spell the word that describes each picture, and then pronounce it. This exercise is intended to illustrate the silent letters and to point up the contrast between the spoken and written language. The answers are:

1. Train (point out that the *ai* has one vowel sound)
2. Kite (point out the silent *e*)
3. Light (point out the silent *gh*)
4. Shoe (some students have difficulty remembering *oe*)
5. Wrist (silent *w*)
6. Comb (silent *b*)
7. Table (silent *e*)
8. Key (silent *y*)
9. Chair (*ai* has one long vowel sound)
10. Thumb (silent *b*)

PRACTICE:

● 1. Review the name of each letter in the alphabet so that the students will be able to say them fluently for spelling practice.

● 2. *Spelling*
Practice words which have "spelling demons" in them, such as silent *e*, silent *gh*, or silent *b*. Some examples of these are listed below.

Silent e	Silent gh	Silent b
kite	right	thumb
gate	light	comb
late	might	
mate	enough	

Write these words on the blackboard. Have the students pronounce the words by repeating them after you, and have them spell each word aloud.

●● 3. *Dictation*
Give a dictation drill using the same words you have reviewed above. Dictate each word twice. Have the students write the word. You may also use the word in short sentences for dictation.

●●● 4. *Discussion*
Lead a discussion about the students' best friends. Call on several students to talk about their best friend, and what they like about this friend. The name of the friend does not have to be mentioned. They may also write a short description of this friend.

ENRICHMENT:

●● 1. *Game: Ghost*
The spelling game *Ghost* would be appropriate to play here. For instructions on how to play the game see page 6 in the ACTIVITY GUIDE for **Who is Sylvia?**

I've Got a Friend Named Fia

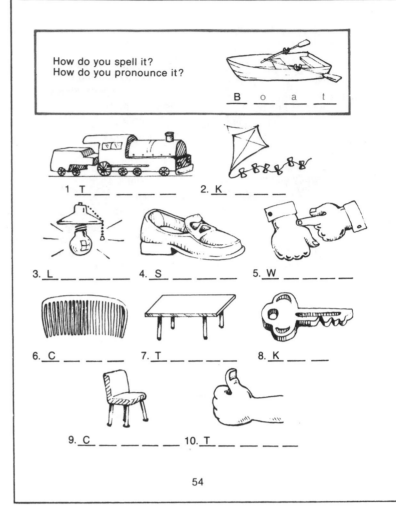

How do you spell it?
How do you pronounce it?

B o a t

1. T _ _ _ _
2. K _ _ _
3. L _ _ _ _
4. S _ _ _
5. W _ _ _ _
6. C _ _ _
7. T _ _ _ _
8. K _ _
9. C _ _ _ _
10. T _ _ _ _

54

●● 2. *Game: I'm thinking of someone or something.*
The student leader thinks of the name of a person or thing. The students try to guess who or what it is by guessing which letters are in the name. For example, they may ask, "Does it have a B?" or "Does it begin with S?"

Each time a student guesses a letter correctly the student leader writes that letter on the blackboard. The object is to finally figure out what the name is. The student who guesses the name correctly, and is able to spell it correctly, wins and becomes the next student leader.

I've Got a Friend Named Fia

I've got a friend named Fia, F I A.
I've got a friend named Fia, F I A.
    How do you spell it?
F I A.
    How do you spell it?
F I A.
    How do you pronounce it?
Fia.
    How do you pronounce it?
Fia.

I've got a friend named Bobby,
B O B B Y.
I've got a friend named Bobby,
B O B B Y.
    How do you spell it?
B O B.
    How do you spell it?
B O B.
    How do you spell it?
B O B, B O B B Y.

    How do you pronounce it?
Bobby.
    How do you pronounce it?
Bobby.

I've got a friend named Annie, A N N I E.
I've got a friend named Annie, A N N I E.
    How do you spell it?
A N N.
    How do you spell it?
A N N.
    How do you pronounce it?
Annie.
    How do you pronounce it?
Annie.
    How do you spell it?

A N N.
A N N, I've got a friend named Annie.
A N N, I've got a friend named Annie.
A N N I E.

CHANT GUIDE

PRONUNCIATION:
This song offers practice in the pronunciation of the names of the letters of the alphabet.

Practice the pronunciation of **friend, named, spell, pronounce,** and **it.**

Listen carefully to the sound of the contraction **I've.**

STRUCTURE:
Notice the use of *I've got,* in place of *I have,* to indicate possession, as it occurs in: **I've got a friend.**

This song is written in the *simple present tense* and offers practice in the frequently used *information questions:* **How do you spell it? How do you pronounce it?**

PRESENTATION:
This music is based on a traditional folk melody. Listen to the accompanying tape for the melody, tempo and style of presentation of this song.

NOTES

_____

_____

_____

_____

_____

_____

_____

_____

_____

_____

_____

ACTIVITY GUIDE

TASK:
Have the students complete the valentine in any way they wish. You might suggest that they write their own messages and decorate or color the page in a spirit appropriate to a valentine.

PRACTICE:
Short Answer Response Forms for Agreement and Disagreement

Have the students practice the various ways of agreeing and disagreeing. They may use the short answer responses practiced in the chant. Sample exercises follow. Before doing any of these exercises, make sure that the students repeat each of the short responses so that their pronunciation is fluent.

● 1. *Affirmative short answer with do*

   T: I like my friends.
   S: So do I, or I do too.
   T: I like ice cream.
   S: So do I, or I do too.

● 2. *Affirmative short answer with be*

   T: I'm cold.
   S: So am I, or I am too.
   T: I'm hungry.
   S: So am I, or I am too.

● 3. *Negative short answer with do*

   T: I don't like my friends.
   S: Neither do I, or I don't either.
   T: I don't like the rain.
   S: Neither do I, or I don't either.

● 4. *Negative short answer with be*

   T: I'm not happy today.
   S: Neither am I, or I'm not either.
   T: I'm not cold today.
   S: Neither am I, or I'm not either.

●● 5. Once the students have had practice responding with each pattern, both *affirmative* with *do* and *be,* and *negative* with *do* and *be,* have them then practice discriminating when to use each pattern response. Either you give the statements or have a student give the statements. An example follows.

   S1: I like ice cream.
   S2: So do I.
   S1: I don't like liver.
   S2: Neither do I.
   S1: I'm tired.
   S2: So am I.
   S1: I'm not thirsty.
   S2: Neither am I.

●●● 6. *Discussion*
   Have the students discuss their real likes and dislikes about various items such as food, sports, music, etc.

I Like My Friends

Make your own valentine.

56

ENRICHMENT:
● 1. *Drawing*
   Have the students draw a picture of something they like or dislike. The more advanced students can write three short reasons why they like or dislike the item that they have drawn.

●● 2. *Opinion Poll*
   Have the more advanced students conduct an opinion poll. Have them make up six questions asking whether the students like a particular item. The more advanced students can ask why the item is liked or disliked. For example: Do you like fish? Why? Why not?

   Let the students who are conducting the poll make up their own questions, then tabulate the answers and report the results to the class. You may have several different students conducting several different opinion polls at once.

I Like My Friends

I like my friends.		I don't like my socks.	
	So do I.		I don't either.
I like my old friends.		I don't like my books.	
	So do I.		I don't either.
I like my new friends.		I don't like my shoes.	
	So do I.		I don't either.
I'm happy today.		I'm not happy today.	
	So am I.		I'm not either.
I don't like my friends.		I like my clothes.	
	Neither do I.		I do too.
I don't like my old friends.		I like my old clothes.	
	Neither do I.		I do too.
I don't like my new friends.		I like my new clothes.	
	Neither do I.		I do too.
I'm not happy today.		I'm happy today.	
	Neither am I.		I am too.

CHANT GUIDE

PRONUNCIATION:
Practice the pronunciation of **neither, either, not, old** and **new.** Practice the contractions: **I'm, don't.**

Listen to the z sound of the plural s ending in **friends, clothes** and **shoes** in contrast to the s sound of the plural ending in **socks** and **books.**

Notice the more explicit pronunciation of the d in do as it occurs in **I do too,** as compared with that of the d in **So do I,** where the do is not emphasized.

STRUCTURE:
This chant offers practice in *simple present tense statements,* both affirmative and negative, using the verbs *be* and *like:*
I'm happy today. I'm not happy today.
I like my friends. I don't like my friends.

It illustrates a pattern of American English which occurs with very high frequency, that of a statement expressing either an affirmative or negative attitude followed by a short response indicating agreement:
I like my friends. So do I.
I'm not happy today. Neither am I.

Notice that two distinct forms are illustrated for the short response: **So do I. / I do too. So am I. / I am too.** Both forms are frequently used by native speakers and carry no measurable difference in meaning.

PRESENTATION:
The accompanying tape provides a model for the presentation of this chant.

NOTES

_____

_____

_____

_____

_____

_____

_____

_____

_____

_____

_____

TASK:

Following the model picture in the example box, have the students say or write on the lines provided the time that they do each activity. Have them also draw in the hands of the clock on each face to match their own written answers. Notice that there may be cultural differences among the students as far as time to have breakfast, lunch and dinner. Students should feel free to express the actual time that they usually do these activities.

PRACTICE:

● 1. *Habitual Present Tense*

Continue asking questions about what time the students or their friends and relatives do things. Use question and answer responses as follows:

T: What time do you (usually) get up?
S: I get up at 7 o'clock, or At 7 o'clock.
T: What time does your mother get up?
S: She gets up at 6 o'clock.

●● 2. *Discussion*

Have students ask each other about what time they do certain activities. They may ask about any appropriate activity with true responses. This question / answer practice will hopefully lead to further discussion about how differently things are done in different cultures.

● 3. *Modal Auxiliaries*

Have students practice, in repetition drill, sentences using *have to, have got to,* and *must* to express necessity and *want* or *don't want* to express desire or lack of it. Some example sentences follow. Have the students repeat them.

I want to eat lunch.
I don't want to eat lunch.
I must eat lunch.
I've got to eat lunch.
I have to eat lunch.

●● 4. *Question and Answer*

Ask students or have the students ask each other what they want to do. Then ask them what they have to do or must do.

Example:

S1: Do you have to go to bed at 10 o'clock?
S2: No, I don't. I have to go to bed at 9 o'clock.
S1: Do you want to go to the dentist?
S2: No. I have to go to the dentist.

Such questions and answers can lead to further discussion of wanting to do things and having to do things. Cultural differences, reflecting different demands on the children, can be brought in here if this develops into a discussion. That is, in some households children have to do more chores or different chores than in others. Let the children tell about their own experiences with regard to what they have to do and what they want to do.

It's Time To Go To Bed

WHAT TIME IS IT?

1. It's time to have lunch.
   It's 12 o'clock.

2. It's time to get up.

3. It's time to have breakfast.

4. It's time to go to school.

5. It's time to do your homework.

6. It's time to go to bed.

58

ENRICHMENT:

● 1. *Telling Time*

Have the students practice using the hands of the clock. This can be done as a group or a whole class activity. Have one student say the time and another student show that time on the hands of the clock. A third student could then write the digits expressing that time on the board.
   Example:

S1: It's 12:30.
S2: Puts the little hand at 12 and the big hand at 6.
S3: Writes 12:30 on the board.

This is continued until the students are familiar with the oral, digital and clock face aspects of telling time.

●● 2. *Discussion*

Have each student relate his or her activities for a typical day from the moment they wake up until the moment they go to sleep, giving the approximate times that they do each activity.

●●● 3. Have students keep a diary for a day, writing down everything they do from the moment they get up until the moment they go to sleep. Have them bring in their diaries and exchange them with other students while they discuss the differences and similarities in their daily routines and how they feel about their day's activities.

It's Time To Go To Bed

It's time to go to bed.
>What time is it?

It's time to go to bed.
>What time is it?

It's time to go to bed.
>I don't want to go to bed.

You have to go to bed.
>What time is it?

You've got to go to bed.
>I don't want to go to bed.

You must go to bed.
>I don't want to go to bed.
>I'm not sleepy,
>I'm not sleepy.

It's time to get up.
>What time is it?

It's time to get up.
>What time is it?

It's time to get up.
>I don't want to get up.

You have to get up.
>I don't want to get up.

You've got to get up.
>I don't want to get up.

You must get up.
>I don't want to get up.
>I don't want to get up.
>I'm sleepy,
>I'm sleepy.

59

CHANT GUIDE

PRONUNCIATION:
Practice the pronunciation of **time, bed, sleepy, get up, not** and the contractions: **it's, don't, you've** and **I'm.**

Listen carefully to the reductions in the sounds of the verbs *got to* (gotta), *have to* (hafta), and *want to* (wanna), when they occur in non-final position in a sentence: **You have to go to bed. You've got to go to bed. I don't want to go to bed.** These reductions are a distinctive feature of American English speech, frequently used by educated native speakers in casual conversation. However, in written and formal communication, *got to, have to* and *want to* are retained.

STRUCTURE:
This chant offers practice in *simple present tense statements* and *questions,* both affirmative and negative, using the verbs **be** and **want.**
Notice the use of the *modal auxiliaries,* **have to, have got to** and **must** to express *necessity.*

PRESENTATION:
The accompanying tape provides a model for the presentation of this chant.

NOTES

ACTIVITY GUIDE

TASK:
Using the circled example, **July,** as a model, have the students circle the names of all of the months in the birthday cake. Then have them write each month in the space provided at the bottom of the page.

PRACTICE:
- 1. Review the months of the year, in order, both orally and in writing on the board. Have the students practice repeating them until they can say them in the correct order as follows:

  January, February, March, April, May, June, July, August, September, October, November, December.

- 2. *Question and Answer*
  Have the students first repeat the example sentences below until they understand the pattern. Then conduct a real question and answer session with the students in the class.

  T: How old are you?
  S: I'm six, or Six.
  T: When are you going to be seven?
  S: I'm going to be seven in October, or In October.

- ● 3. *Vocabulary*
  Introduce vocabulary for different occupations so that students may use this vocabulary in the practice exercises below to talk about what they're going to be.

farmer	musician	veterinarian
dentist	secretary	shop keeper
doctor	baker	fire chief
banker	dancer	police officer
nurse	baseball player	barber
teacher	football player	carpenter
engineer	scientist	plumber
mechanic	actress / actor	pilot
lawyer	poet	butcher

- ● 3. *Future with going to*
  Encourage the students to talk about *what* they're going to be when they're adults and *where* they're going to be. Use the following question and answer patterns.

  T: What are you going to be when you're twenty-two?
  S1: I'm going to be a doctor.
  T: What are you going to be when you're twenty-two?
  S2: I'm going to be a lawyer.
  T: Where are you going to be when you're twenty-two?
  S1: I might be in Tokyo.
  T: Where are you going to be when you're twenty-two?
  S2: I might be in Mexico.

  Encourage the students to go beyond these question and answer patterns into a discussion of what they think they will be doing with their lives in the future.

What Are You Going To Do When You're Twenty-Two?

1. _____July_____ 2. _____ 3. _____
4. _____ 5. _____ 6. _____
7. _____ 8. _____ 9. _____
10. _____ 11. _____ 12. _____

60

ENRICHMENT:
- 1. *Drawing*
  Have the students draw a picture of an activity that they are going to do on their next birthday. Have them write what month it will be and a one sentence description of the activity.

- ● ● 2. Have the students tell about the profession they are most interested in. Have them either bring in a picture or draw a picture of a person in their chosen profession. Have them write what that person does and why they want to have that occupation when they grow up.

What Are You Going To Do When You're Twenty-Two?

What are you going to do when you're twenty-two?
>I haven't decided.
>What about you?

I might climb a mountain.
I might go to France.
I might write a story.
I might learn to dance.

Where are you going to be when you're twenty-three?
>I might be in Paris.
>I might be in Rome.
>I might be in Turkey.
>I might be home.

What are you going to be when you're ninety-three?
>I'm going to be old
>when I'm ninety-three.

What are you going to do when you're one hundred and two?
>I haven't decided.
>What about you?

61

CHANT GUIDE

PRONUNCIATION:
Practice the pronunciation of **twenty-two, decided, about, might, climb, mountain, ninety-three,** and **one hundred and two.**
Practice the sound of the contractions: **you're, haven't, I'm.**

Listen to the reduction in the sound of *going to* (gonna) when it occurs in non-final position in a question, **What are you going to do?** or a statement, **I'm going to be old.** This reduction is a distinctive feature of American English speech, frequently used by educated native speakers in casual conversation. However, in written and formal communication, *going to* is retained.

STRUCTURE:
This poem illustrates a useful combination of structures frequently found in American English speech. The first speaker opens with a question in the *future* with *be + going to,* **What are you going to do?** answered by a response in the *present perfect,* **I haven't decided.** The original question is then returned to the first speaker, using the expression, **What about you?**

Notice the use of the *modal auxiliary might* to express possibility: **I might climb a mountain.**

The poem also provides practice in the use of *in* as a *preposition of place* referring to a city, **in Rome,** or a country, **in Turkey.**

PRESENTATION:
See page ix for suggestions on presenting the poems.

NOTES

ACTIVITY GUIDE

TASK:
Have the students trace their way from the **Start Here** arrow to the building labeled, **My friend's house.** Have them write or say the names of five things that they saw along the way.

PRACTICE:
● 1. Using the picture as a reference, have individual students name additional things that they found in the picture.

●● 2. *Discussion*
Ask individual students to describe a trip to their friend's house or to some other place. Ask them the following questions:

How long does it take to get there?
What do you see along the way?

This can lead to interesting discussions about places in the neighborhood and the students' concepts of time.

●● 3. Students may want to know that the amount of money in the chant comes to $15.36. It might be interesting to see if any students can figure this out for themselves.

Explain the relationships among various U.S. coins. Explain that five pennies equal a nickel, two nickels equal a dime, two dimes plus a nickel equal a quarter, five nickels equal a quarter and four quarters equal a dollar. Have students practice these relationships verbally by asking the following questions:

S1: How much is two dimes and a nickel?
S2: A quarter.
S1: How much is five pennies?
S2: A nickel.

You can use money made out of cardboard or play money to illustrate the meaning.

●● 4. *Question and Answer*
Have the students ask and answer, to the best of their ability, how much it costs to buy a candy bar or how much it costs to buy a hamburger. The students should answer, "It costs 25¢ to buy a candy bar." or "It costs 75¢ to buy a hamburger." Be sure they have the final *s* on *costs*. The teacher can cue which items the students are asking the price of. Choose items that the students come in contact with frequently, such as candy, food, games, toys.

ENRICHMENT:
1. *Role Play*
Have the students set up cardboard boxes representing different kinds of stores: a grocery store, a drug store, a bakery, fruit store. Have them cut out or make pictures of typical items sold in each store, and label each item with a price. Have the students use play money, or make play money, to pay for their purchases.

I'm Thinking About Tomorrow

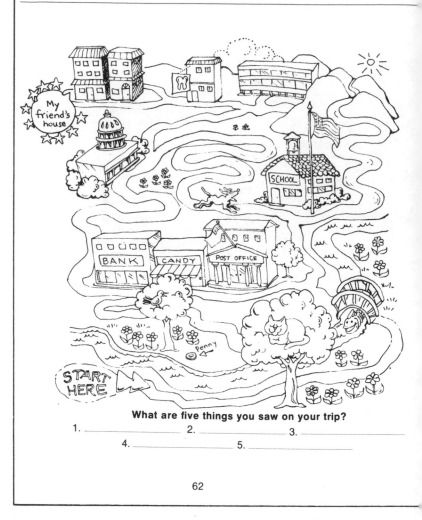

What are five things you saw on your trip?
1. _____   2. _____   3. _____
4. _____   5. _____

62

Have some students be the customers and other students be the store keepers. Have the students practice using language such as:

"Do you have any . . . ?" "How much does it cost?" and "It costs. . . ."

Have the students practice making change.

This project could develop over several days or even several weeks.

62

I'm Thinking About Tomorrow

What? What?
What are you doing?
What are you doing now?
> Thinking, I'm thinking.
> Thinking, I'm thinking.

What are you thinking about?
> I'm thinking about tomorrow, tomorrow, tomorrow.
> I'm going to take a trip tomorrow.
> It's going to be a beautiful day.

Where? Where?
Where are you going?
Where? Where?
Where are you going?
> I'm going to see a friend of mine.

When? When?
When are you leaving?
> I'm leaving at a quarter to nine.

How long does it take to get there, to get there, to get there?
How long does it take to get there?
> A long, long time.
> It takes 14 years, 7 months, 13 hours and a minute and a half.
> 14 years, 7 months, 13 hours and a minute and a half.

How long does it take to get there?
> A long, long time.

How much does it cost to get there?
How much does it cost to get there?
> It costs a lot, it costs a lot.
> It costs 14 dollars, 7 dimes, 13 nickels and a penny.
> 14 dollars, 7 dimes, 13 nickels and a penny.

63

CHANT GUIDE

PRONUNCIATION:
Practice the pronunciation of the question words:
What? Where? When? How long? How much?
Practice the contractions: **I'm, it's.**
Practice the pronunciation of **now, about, tomorrow, trip, beautiful, mine, month, minute and a half, dollar, dime, nickel** and **penny.**

Listen to the -*ing* endings in **doing, thinking, going** and **leaving.**
Listen for the third person *s* in **takes** and **costs.** Notice the *z* sound of the plural *s* in **years, hours, dimes** and **nickels** in contrast with the *s* sound in **months.**

Notice the reduction in the sound of *going to* (gonna) when it occurs in non-final position in a sentence: **I'm going to take a trip.** This reduction is a distinctive feature of American English speech, frequently used by educated native speakers in casual conversation. However, in written and formal communication, *going to* is retained.

STRUCTURE:
This song includes examples of the *question* and *statement pattern* in the *present continuous tense:* **What are you doing now? I'm thinking about tomorrow;** the *future statement* with *be + going to:* **I'm going to take a trip tomorrow;** and the *simple present question* and *statement:* **How long does it take? It takes. . . .**

It also illustrates the use of the *present continuous tense* to express future time: **I'm leaving at a quarter to nine.**

This song provides practice in the question words: **What? Where? When? How long? How much?**

It includes words and expressions for vocabulary development relating to time and money: **a quarter to, a long time, now, tomorrow, year, month, hour, minute and a half, a lot, dollar, dime, nickel** and **penny.**

PRESENTATION:
Listen to the accompanying tape for the melody, tempo and style of presentation of this song.

NOTES

_____

_____

_____

_____

_____

_____

_____

_____

_____

_____

_____

_____

_____

ACTIVITY GUIDE

TASK:
Using the example box as a model, have the students say or write the name of each object in the space provided above the object. For example, A **bike** is smaller than a **car.** When the sentence is completed, have the students check the appropriate box on the right. The first statement is a true statement, so the students check **Right.** The second statement in the example box when completed, A **car** is smaller than a **bike,** is an incorrect statement, so the students check **Wrong.** Have the students complete the rest of the sentences in the same manner. The final page should read as follows:

1. A **bus** is faster than a **plane.**   **Wrong**
2. A **bed** is softer than a **table.**   **Right**
3. An **apple** is sweeter than a **lemon.**   **Right**
4. A **tree** is taller than a **flower.**   **Right**
5. A **bathtub** is bigger than a **sink.**   **Right**
6. A **train** is slower than a **horse.**   **Wrong**
7. A **clock** is larger than a **watch.**   **Right**
8. A **blackboard** is smaller than an **eraser.**   **Wrong**

PRACTICE:

● 1. *Vocabulary*
   Review the comparative vocabulary presented in the picture. Have the students repeat words like faster, softer, sweeter, taller, bigger, slower, larger, smaller. Then introduce the uninflected form and the superlative form for each one. Example: fast / fastest; soft / softest; sweet / sweetest; tall / tallest; big / biggest; slow / slowest; large / largest; small / smallest.

   Then ask the students to supply words that describe something (adjectives), and have them put the comparative and superlative endings on them.

   S1: Tall, taller, tallest.
   S2: Short, shorter, shortest.

●● 2. Present several sets of objects to the class in groups of two. Have the students describe them using the comparative adjectives you have just reviewed. For example:

   T: How are these different? (Holding up a pencil and a ribbon.)
   S1: The pencil is harder.
   S2: The ribbon is softer.
   S3: The pencil is bigger.
   S4: The ribbon is smaller.

●● 3. Present three or more items. Have the students identify the superlative in each case. For example, present a tree, a leaf and an apple.

   T: Which is the biggest?
   S1: The tree.
   T: Which is the smallest?
   S2: The leaf.
   T: Which is the best to eat?
   S3: The apple.

I'm Always Right

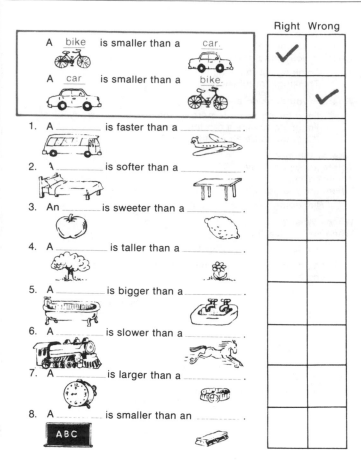

64

●●● 4. *Discussion*
   Have a discussion about being right and being wrong. Have the students give one example of when they were right about something and one example of when they were wrong about something.

   If the students are advanced enough, ask if they think it's important for them to be right. If they do, ask why. If they don't, ask why not.

ENRICHMENT:

●● 1. *Game*
   Have each student write down a simple prediction about a future event. It could be a prediction about the weather, or the particular food that they will have for lunch, or what somebody will wear to class.

   Have them write on an envelope the date on which they think the prediction will come true. Seal the prediction inside the envelope. When that date arrives, open the envelope and see whether the prediction was right or wrong.

I'm Always Right

I'm right,	Clap, Clap
I'm always right.	
I'm right,	Clap, Clap
I'm always right.	
You're wrong,	Clap, Clap
You're always wrong.	
You're wrong,	Clap, Clap
You're always wrong.	
Sometimes I'm wrong.	
That's right.	Clap, Clap
Sometimes I'm wrong.	
That's right.	Clap, Clap
You're always wrong.	
I'm right.	Clap, Clap
You're always wrong.	
I'm right.	Clap, Clap

CHANT GUIDE

PRONUNCIATION:
Practice the pronunciation of the contractions: **I'm, you're, that's.**

Listen to the *z* sound of the final *s* in **always** and **sometimes.**

STRUCTURE:
This chant provides practice in the *simple present tense statements:* **I'm always right. You're wrong.**

It also illustrates the use of the *frequency words,* **always** and **sometimes.**

PRESENTATION:
Conduct this chant with a strict, military beat. The accompanying tape provides a model for the presentation of this chant.

NOTES

_____

_____

_____

_____

_____

_____

_____

_____

_____

_____

_____

ACTIVITY GUIDE

TASK:

Using the example as a model, have the students complete each question either orally or by writing in the blank spaces provided at the right of each picture. The questions with the appropriate answers are listed below.

1. Who's going? — Bill
2. Where's he going? — To the playground or to the baseball field.

3. Who's going? — Sally
4. Where's she going? — To the library.
5. Who's going? — Jim
6. Where's he going? — To the movies.
7. Who's going? — Annie
8. Where's she going? — To school.

PRACTICE:

● 1. Have the students repeat the questions used in the chant and the activities with appropriate answers.

    T: Who's going? Bill's going. (Students repeat.)
    T: Where's he going? To the playground. (Students repeat.)
    T: When's he going? At a quarter after three. (Students repeat.)
    T: What's he going to do at the playground? Play ball. (Students repeat.)

    Continue with additional models of this type and have the students repeat.

●● 2. *Statement plus Question and Answer Practice*
Provide a model sentence for the students which will give the information about who, where, and when. Then ask the *Who, Where* and *When* questions for each statement, and have the students give the appropriate answers. Example:

    T: John's going to the park at 4:30.
    T: Who's going?
    S1: John
    T: Where's he going?
    S2: To the park.
    T: When's he going?
    S3: At 4:30.
    T: Mary's going to the library at a quarter to two.
    T: Who's going?
    S4: Mary
    T: Where's she going?
    S5: To the library.
    T: When's she going?
    S6: At a quarter to two.

●● 3. *Vocabulary*
Have the students repeat the vocabulary for food that one can buy at the grocery store. A suggested list follows:

milk	hamburger	cheese
eggs	bread	meat
fish	cookies	pears
bananas	apples	tomatoes
oranges	pineapple	peas
beans	lettuce	hot dogs
pepper	chicken	cereal

Grandma's Going to the Grocery Store

Who's going?
Where's she going?
    Grandma
    to the grocery store

1. Who's going? _____
2. Where's he going? _____

3. Who's going? _____
4. Where's she going? _____

5. Who's going? _____
6. Where's he going? _____

7. Who's going? _____
8. Where's she going? _____

66

●●● 4. *Question and Answer*
Ask the students, "What do you like to buy at the grocery store?" Have the students respond freely with their own answers. This may lead to an interesting discussion of likes and dislikes and cultural differences. This practice exercise may be expanded depending on the vocabulary level of the students. You could ask, for example:
What do you like to buy at the drug store?
What do you like to buy at the department store?
What do you like to buy at the toy store?

ENRICHMENT:

● 1. Have the students make clocks out of cardboard and practice showing the time on their clocks. For example: 2:15, 2:30, a quarter to three, three o'clock. Depending on the level of sophistication of the students, they could also practice 2:20, 2:23, 2:25.

●● 2. *Game: Add a Word*
This game tests the student's vocabulary as well as his memory. Have the first student begin a sentence as follows: "I'm going to the grocery store to buy a can of peas."

    The next student must repeat what the first student said and add what he will buy. For example:

Grandma's Going to the Grocery Store

Grandma's going to the grocery store.
>One, two, three, four.

Grandma's going to the grocery store.
>One, two, three, four.

Who's going?
>Grandma's going.

Who's going?
>Grandma's going.

Where's she going?
>To the grocery store.
>One, two, three, four.

When's she going?
>At a quarter after four.
>One, two, three, four.

What's she going to buy at the grocery store?
>One, two, three, four.

What's she going to buy at the grocery store?
>One, two, three, four.

A loaf of bread,
a bottle of milk,
a big bag of cookies
and a little can of peas.
>A loaf of bread,
>a bottle of milk,
>a big bag of cookies
>and a little can of peas.

Grandma's going to the grocery store.
>One, two, three, four.

Grandma's going to the grocery store.
>One, two, three, four.

67

"I'm going to the grocery store to buy a can of peas and a bag of cookies."

The next student continues the chain and adds another item. For example: "I'm going to the grocery store to buy a can of peas, a bag of cookies and a bottle of milk."

The game is continued until the chain is broken by a student who cannot remember all the items or who makes a mistake. That student then starts a new sentence and the game is repeated again, using different vocabulary.

CHANT GUIDE

PRONUNCIATION:
Practice the pronunciation of the contractions. Notice the z sound of the final s in **Grandma's, who's, where's** and **when's** in contrast with the s sound in **what's.**

Practice the pronunciation of the numbers **one, two, three** and **four.** Notice that the intonation pattern here is the one used to indicate a *series* of items. There's a slight rise in intonation in the penultimate item in the series. In this case, the rise comes on the word **three.**

Practice the intonation patterns of the information question, **Who's going?** and the response, **Grandma's going.** Notice that the rise in intonation on *who's* in **Who's going?** implies a need for *clarification* of the subject in the original statement.

Listen to the reduction in the sound of *going to* (gonna) when it occurs in non-final position in a sentence: **What's she going to buy?** This reduction is a distinctive feature of American English speech, frequently used by educated native speakers in casual conversation. However, in written and formal communication, *going to* is retained.

STRUCTURE:
This chant provides practice in the *present continuous statement,* **Grandma's going to the grocery store;** followed by *information questions* with **Who, Where, When** and **What.**

It illustrates the use of the *present continuous tense* to express both immediate *present* and *future time.* The statement, **Grandma's going to the grocery store,** could describe an action taking place at that moment and witnessed by the speaker or it could refer to a future intention. The question, **When's she going?** could imply a future time.

This chant includes repeated examples of the use of the *definite* and *indefinite articles,* **the grocery store, a loaf of bread;** and a wide variety of useful words and expressions for vocabulary development: **a loaf of bread, a bottle of milk, a big bag of cookies, a little can of peas.**

PRESENTATION:
The accompanying tape provides a model for the presentation of this chant.

NOTES

ACTIVITY GUIDE

TASK:

Have the students fill in, with pencil, ink or crayon, the appropriate design which matches the top for each set of pajamas.

PRACTICE:

● 1. *Vocabulary:* Adjectives

Have students practice with a variety of adjectives which are both in the chant and in the activity. A suggested list of adjectives follows.

striped	polka dot	plaid
checked	nice	pretty
beautiful	ugly	tiny
big	little	red
blue	green	yellow
black	white	brown
comfortable	soft	hard

● 2. *Vocabulary:* Nouns

Have students practice the vocabulary for common household objects and clothing. It is helpful to introduce these words by using pictures from magazines which illustrate the words, and then having the students repeat the words. A suggested list follows.

skirt	blouse	pants
socks	shoes	jumper
dress	jacket	coat
sweater	T-shirt	suit
drawer	bed	door
floor	pillow	room
kitchen	living room	house

● ● 3. Have students practice combining the adjective and noun combinations they have previously learned in **Practice 1** and **2** above. Have them use the model sentence: "I have (a) _____ _____." Each student may orally provide the appropriate combination. For example:

I have a *red dress.* I have a *striped jacket.*
I have *polka dot pajamas.* I have *beautiful clothes.*
I have a *big house.* I have a *small house.*

To make this more interesting, the teacher can list the adjectives on the board and then the nouns and point to possible combinations. Or the teacher may use pictures of colors and patterns for adjectives, and pictures of the objects mentioned for nouns, to cue the students.

● ● 4. Have students practice with adjective plus noun combinations, as above, using two adjectives plus a noun.

For example: Great big door. Nice little room.

Polka Dot Pajamas

68

ENRICHMENT:

● ● 1. *Drawing*

Have students draw pictures illustrating adjective plus noun combinations. When the pictures are done, have the students exchange their pictures and describe what they see, using as many adjectives plus noun combinations, as possible. For example: Pretty red skirt; red polka dot pajamas; tiny little cat.

● ● 2. Have students pantomime their activities in the morning, and have the other students describe the activity that is being pantomimed, using the past tense, as it is modeled in the chant. For example:

"I got out of bed, jumped on the pillow, stood on my head, took off my pajamas. . . ."

Polka Dot Pajamas

I woke up early,
早early in the morning
Got out of bed,
　　comfortable bed
Jumped on the pillow,
　　soft pillow
Stood on my head,
　　hard head
Took off my pajamas,
　　polka dot pajamas
Put on my clothes,
　　beautiful clothes
Brushed my teeth,
　　nice white teeth
Blew my nose,
　　tiny little nose
Had my breakfast,
　　great big breakfast

Fed the cat,
　　fat cat
Went back to my room,
　　nice little room
Opened the door,
　　great big door
Saw my pajamas,
　　polka dot pajamas
On the floor,
　　polka dot pajamas
Picked them up,
　　polka dot pajamas
Put them in a drawer,
　　polka dot pajamas
Picked up my books,
　　three or four
Said goodbye to Mama,
And ran out the door.

CHANT GUIDE

PRONUNCIATION:
Practice the pronunciation of **woke, got, out, of, off, soft, comfortable, beautiful, clothes, nose, back, fat, cat, fed, nice, white, floor** and **drawer.**

Listen to the *s* sound of the plural *s* in **books** and the *z* sound of the plural *s* in **pajamas.**

Notice the *t* sound of the past tense ending in **jumped, brushed** and **picked.**
Notice the final *th* sound in **teeth.**

STRUCTURE:
This chant provides practice in a wide variety of *regular* and *irregular verbs* in the *simple past tense*.

Notice the two-word verbs: **woke up, got out, jumped on, stood on, took off, put on, went back, picked up, put in, ran out.**

This chant introduces high frequency words and expressions useful for vocabulary development. It gives particular practice with adjectives: **comfortable, soft, hard, beautiful, nice, tiny, great, big.**
It also provides practice with vocabulary indicating parts of the body: **teeth, nose, head;** and familiar household objects: **bed, room, floor, drawer.**

PRESENTATION:
The accompanying tape provides a model for the presentation of this chant.

NOTES

ACTIVITY GUIDE

TASK:
Following the example of the circled word **doctor**, have the students circle the hidden words in the puzzle and write them in the spaces provided. The hidden words are: **doctor, back, his, hand, eye, sick, old, is, arm, nurse, the.** You may extend this activity by then having the students use these words in sentences. For example: The old doctor is sick, or The doctor is old.

PRACTICE:

- 1. *Vocabulary*
  Practice words to describe aches and pains as suggested by the chant and the activity. A list follows:

headache	fever	blister
stomachache	backache	toothache
cold	sore throat	cough

- 2. Have + *got*
  Have the students look at the drawings of sick animals and children on the Activity Page and describe what is wrong. Use the structure of *have + got.* For example: *He's got a fever.* This is a contraction of *he has got a fever.* Clockwise on the activity page, the answers are as follows:

  He's got a fever.
  He's got a toothache.
  She's got a backache.
  He's got a toothache.
  He's got a cold.
  She's got a stomachache.
  The cat feels terrible.

  Continue this practice by having the students give their own sentences using I've, She's, He's or They've *got a* fever / cold / headache / etc. Note that one can also say, *He has a toothache,* instead of *has got.*

- ● 3. *Discussion*
  Have the students mention an ailment and a suggested cure for it. For example:

  S1: I've got a headache.
  S2: Take an aspirin.
  S3: I've got a fever.
  S4: Go to bed.
  S5: I've got a toothache.
  S6: Go to the dentist.

  This can lead to further elaboration depending on the language level of the students.

ENRICHMENT:

- ● 1 Have individual students pantomime an ache or pain, and have other students describe it. Gestures are suggested by the pictures on the Activity Page.

- ● 2. Have the students draw a picture of themselves having an ache or pain and the solution or cure for that particular ache or pain. For example: A picture of a student with a toothache and then that same student at the dentist.

I Feel Terrible

1. <u>doctor</u>   2. _____   3. _____   4. _____

5. _____   6. _____   7. _____   8. _____

70

NOTES

_____

_____

_____

_____

_____

_____

_____

_____

_____

_____

_____

_____

I Feel Terrible

I've got a headache.
I've got a headache.
I don't want to go to bed.

I've got a fever.
I've got a fever.
I don't want to do my homework.

I've got a stomachache.
I've got a stomachache.
I don't want to eat my lunch.

I've got a blister.
I've got a blister.
I don't want to see my sister.

Every time I get a headache,
Mama takes me to the doctor.

Every time I get a fever,
Mama takes me to the nurse.

Every time I get a toothache,
Mama takes me to the dentist.

Every time I see the dentist,
I always come home feeling worse.

I've got a headache.
I've got a headache.
I don't want to go to bed.

I've got a fever.
I've got a fever.
I don't want to do my homework.

I've got a stomachache.
I've got a stomachache.
I don't want to eat my lunch.

I've got a blister.
I've got a blister.
I don't want to see my sister.

71

CHANT GUIDE

PRONUNCIATION:
Practice the pronunciation of **got, homework, fever, blister, sister, doctor, nurse, dentist, feeling** and **worse.**
Practice the contractions: **I've, don't.**

Listen to the *k* sound of the *ch* in **headache, stomachache** and **toothache** in contrast with the *ch* sound of the *ch* in **lunch.**
Listen for the *s* sound of the third person *s* in **takes.**

Notice the reduction in the sound of *want to* (wanna) when it occurs in non-final position in a sentence: **I don't want to do my homework.** This reduction is a distinctive feature of American English speech, frequently used by educated native speakers in casual conversation. However, in written and formal communication, *want to* is retained.

STRUCTURE:
This chant is written in the *simple present tense* using affirmative and negative statements: **I've got a headache. I don't want to go to bed.**

It illustrates the *third person s* as it occurs in **Mama takes me;** and the use of the frequency words *always* and *every time* as they occur in: **Every time I see . . . , I always come home. . . .**

Notice the use of *have got* in place of *have* to indicate possession: **I've got.** In American English, one can use *have got* (I've got, she's got, he's got), or simply *have* (I have, she has, he has), to indicate a *condition* or *possession.*

PRESENTATION:
This song is based on the folk melody, "La Cucaracha." Listen to the accompanying tape for the melody, tempo and style of presentation of this song.

NOTES

_____

_____

_____

_____

_____

_____

_____

_____

_____

_____

ACTIVITY GUIDE

TASK:
Using the example as a model, have the students write or tell *who* didn't like *what* in each picture. The answers follow:

1. The dog didn't like the cat.
2. The cat didn't like the bird.
3. The dog didn't like the house.
4. The bird didn't like the cage.

PRACTICE:
● 1. Have the students repeat the sentences illustrated by the pictures on the Activity Page (listed above). Have them point to the appropriate picture as they say each sentence. Example: The dog (point to the dog) didn't like the cat (point to the cat).

● 2. *Who Questions to Determine Subject*
Practice *Who questions* with the students to make sure that they understand and can identify the subject of each sentence on the Activity Page. Use random order.

T: Who didn't like the cat?
S: The dog.
T: Who didn't like the cage?
S: The bird.
T: Who didn't like the bird?
S: The cat.
T: Who didn't like the house?
S: The dog.

If the students need it, continue this type of practice by giving the students additional sentences and then asking them *Who questions.*

●●● 3. *What Questions to Determine Object*
Practice *What questions* with the students to make sure they understand and can identify the object of these same sentences on the Activity Page. Use random order.

T: What didn't the bird like?
S: The cage.
T: What didn't the cat like?
S: The bird.
T: What didn't the dog like?
S: The house, or The cat.

Notice that the last question may have two possible answers according to the pictures, since the objects of sentence 1 and 3 are different. If the students give both answers, it shows that they really understand the practice. If they give only one answer, point out the other.
Continue this with other sentences.

●●● 4. *Who and What Questions*
Alternate *Who* and *What questions* as indicated in **Practice 2** and **3** above until the students achieve some fluency in being able to answer each of these.

I Bought a Dog for My Cat

The cat didn't like the dog.

1. _____

2. _____

3. _____

4. _____

72

ENRICHMENT:
● 1. *Drawing*
Have the students draw a picture of the pet that they would like to have or that they do have.

●● 2. *Discussion*
Have the students discuss which animals they like and which they don't like.

●●● 3. Have the students do or make something *for* someone else in the class and then have them tell what they did or made and why. Example:

S1: I made a picture for John because I have new crayons.
S2: I made a picture for John because I like him.
S3: I bought a candy bar for Lisa because she gave me a cookie.

I Bought a Dog for My Cat

I bought a dog for my cat.
    The cat didn't like the dog.   Meow!

I bought a bird for my cat.
    The cat didn't like the bird.   Meow!

I bought a house for the dog.
    The dog didn't like the house.   Grrr!

I bought a cage for the bird.
    The bird didn't like the cage.   Peep!

The cat didn't like the dog.   Meow!
The dog didn't like the cat.   Grrr!

Nobody liked the bird.   Peep!
    Nobody liked the bird.   Peep!

73

CHANT GUIDE

PRONUNCIATION:
Practice the pronunciation of **bought, dog, cat, didn't, bird, cage** and **nobody.**

Listen to the *t* sound in the final past tense ending of **liked.**

STRUCTURE:
This chant provides practice in *simple past tense* affirmative and negative statements: **I bought a dog. The cat didn't like the dog.**

It illustrates the use of the *definite* and *indefinite articles:* **I bought a dog for my cat. The cat didn't like the dog.**

PRESENTATION:
The accompanying tape provides a model for the presentation of this chant.

NOTES

ACTIVITY GUIDE

TASK:

Have the students circle the hidden words in the picture and write at least eight of them in the spaces provided at the bottom of the page. The first word, **stop,** is done as an example. The following words are hidden in the picture: **stop, in, my, me, bothering, you, I, the, please, tease, am, to, not, go,** and **he.**

Have the students write or say as many sentences as possible using these words. Some examples follow:

Please stop bothering me.
You tease me.
Please stop.
I am not bothering you.

PRACTICE:

● 1. *Vocabulary*
   Introduce and practice various action verbs in the present continuous such as: whispering, giggling, laughing, running, jumping, singing, dancing, writing, drawing, scratching. Have the students perform the action as they practice each word.

●● 2. Have the students divide into groups of two to practice *the accusing command, the denial,* and *the argumentative short response* as demonstrated in the chant. This can be done effectively when several groups of two are doing this simultaneously.

   An example of the routine for each group of two students follows:

   S1: Performs an action. (whispers)
   S2: Stop whispering. (accusing command)
   S1: I'm not whispering. (denial)
   S2: Yes, you are. (argumentative short response)
   S1: No, I'm not. (argumentative short response)
   S2: Yes, you are.
   S1: No, I'm not.
   This may be continued further by using the *emphatic forms:*
   S2: You are too.
   S1: I am not.

ENRICHMENT:

● 1. Drawing
   Have the students draw a picture of somebody doing something which bothers them.

●●● 2. *Discussion*
   Have the students talk about something that a friend or relative does which bothers them. Bring out the importance of respecting people's personal feelings and cultural differences.

Go Away!

1. ___stop___ 2. _____ 3. _____ 4. _____

5. _____ 6. _____ 7. _____ 8. _____

74

NOTES

_____

_____

_____

_____

_____

_____

_____

_____

_____

_____

_____

_____

Go Away!

Go away!
        What?
Go away!
Stop bothering me!
        I'm not bothering you.
Yes, you are.
        No, I'm not.
Yes, you are.
        No, I'm not.
You are too.
        I am not.
You are too.
        I am not.
You do it all the time.
        I do not.
Yes, you do.
        No, I don't.
Yes, you do.
        No, I don't.

You do too.
        I do not.
You do too.
        I do not.
You're just like your sister.
        I am not.
Yes, you are.
        No, I'm not.
Yes, you are.
        No, I'm not.
She does it all the time.
        No, she doesn't.
Yes, she does.
        No, she doesn't.
Go away!
Go away!
Stop bothering me!

CHANT GUIDE

PRONUNCIATION:
Practice the pronunciation of **stop, bothering, just, not, sister** and the sound of the contractions: **I'm, don't, you're, doesn't.**

Listen to the intonation pattern of the one-word question, **What?**

Notice the change in rhythm and stress in the emphatic, **You are too; I am not.**

STRUCTURE:
This chant provides practice in a high frequency pattern of American English conversation, an *accusing command,* **Stop bothering me,** followed by a *present continuous* statement of *denial,* **I'm not bothering you.**

It offers repeated examples of the *short argumentative pattern:* **Yes, you are. No, I'm not; Yes, you do. No, I don't; Yes, she does. No, she doesn't.** Notice the inclusion of the *emphatic forms:* **You are too. You do too.**

This chant illustrates the use of the *subject pronouns* **I, you, she;** the *object pronouns* **me, you;** and introduces the expressions **all the time** and **just like.**

PRESENTATION:
The accompanying tape provides a model for the presentation of this chant.

NOTES

ACTIVITY GUIDE

TASK:

Have the students study the map and answer the questions in the space provided, as shown in the example. Repeat the general question each time: **Where will Tom go if . . . ?** The possible answers follow:

1. He'll go to the post office.
2. He'll go to the library.
3. He'll go to the dentist, or He'll go to the movies.
4. He'll go to the swimming pool.

PRACTICE:

● ● 1. *Real Conditional*

Have the students continue practicing the *real conditional* used in the chant. Provide the substitute verbs as cues in a simple substitution drill.

T: If she <u>goes</u>, I'll go too.
T: sings
S: If she sings, I'll sing too.
T: walks
S: If she walks, I'll walk too.

● ● 2. Continue with a substitution drill similar to the one above. This time, however, change the pattern slightly and have the students practice substituting the correct forms of verbs, subjects and objects.

T: If you sing, I'll sing along with you.
T: he
S: If he sings, I'll sing along with him.
T: dances
S: If he dances, I'll dance along with him.
T: she
S: If she dances, I'll dance along with her.

ENRICHMENT:

● ● 1. *Game*

Have each student print a fairly simple command on a large cardboard sign and, using string, hang the sign around his neck. The command should indicate an action. For example:

Pick up the pencil.
Scratch your ear.
Hop on your right foot.
Smile.

All students should be wearing their signs in order to play the game. Divide the students into two teams.

Using the action commands as cues, each student, in turn, performs the action indicated on his card, while using the real conditional to describe his own and his teammates' actions. The game proceeds as follows: Student 1 performs an action. Student 2 describes the action of Student 1, and his own action, using the real conditional. Student 1 must keep performing his action until Student 2 has responded correctly.

If You Go, I'll Go

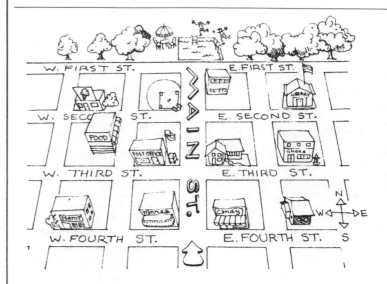

WHERE WILL TOM GO?

He turns right on East Fourth Street.   He'll go to the candy store.

1. He turns left on West Third Street. _____

2. He turns right on East Second Street and walks two blocks.
   _____

3. He turns left on West Fourth Street. _____

4. He walks to the end of Main street. _____

76

This is continued as a chain. The team that can carry it out the longest and is most often correct wins. An example follows:

S1: (scratches his ear)
S2: If you scratch your ear, I'll hop on my right foot. (hops)
S3: If John scratches his ear, and Mary hops on her right foot (John does so and Mary does so until **S3** says), I'll pick up the pencil.

If You Go, I'll Go

If you go, I'll go,
I'll go with you.
    If you go, I'll go,
    I'll go along with you.
If you go, I'll go, I'll go too.
    If you go, I'll go too,
    I'll go along with you.
If she goes, I'll go, I'll go too.
    If she goes, I'll go,
    I'll go along with her.
If she goes, I'll go, I'll go too.
    If she goes, I'll go,
    I'll go along with you.
If he goes, I'll go, I'll go too.
    If he goes, I'll go,
    I'll go along with him.
If he goes, I'll go, I'll go too.
    If he goes, I'll go,
    I'll go along with you.
If they go, we'll go, we'll go too.
    If they go, we'll go,
    We'll go along with them.
If they go, we'll go, we'll go too.
    We'll go along with you.

CHANT GUIDE

PRONUNCIATION:
Practice the pronunciation of **with, along, them** and the sound of the contractions: **I'll, we'll.**

Listen to the *z* sound of the third person *es* ending in **goes.**

STRUCTURE:
This song provides practice in the *real conditional statement:* **If you go, I'll go; If she goes, I'll go.**

It illustrates the use of the *subject pronouns:* **I, you, she, he, we, they;** the *object pronouns:* **her, him, you, them;** and introduces the expression **to go along with.**

PRESENTATION:
Listen to the accompanying tape for the melody, tempo and style of presentation of this song.

NOTES

ACTIVITY GUIDE

TASK:
Have the students look at each picture and indicate whether the item is usually hot or cold by marking a check in the appropriate box. The answers appear below.

PRACTICE:

●● 1. Using the Activity Page, have the students say each picture sentence aloud as follows:

1. Snow is cold.
2. Soup is hot.
3. Ice cream is cold.
4. The sun is hot.
5. Coffee (or tea) is hot.
6. Rain is cold.
7. Ice is cold.
8. Fire is hot.

●● 2. *Vocabulary*
Introduce other simple descriptive adjectives like hot and cold. A suggested list follows:

cool	slippery	fuzzy
warm	wet	shiny
soft	dry	dull
hard		

●● 3. Using the simple pattern, *Be + Noun + Adjective,* as in, "Is snow cold?", practice real questions and answers with the students, asking information about familiar objects.

T: Is toast wet?
S: No. It's dry.
T: Is the ocean hot?
S: No. It's cold.
T: Is ice slippery?
S: Yes, it is.

This may be continued with student-to-student questions and answers.

You may need to introduce the words *usually, sometimes* and *always.*

ENRICHMENT:

●● 1. *Drawing*
Introduce the concept of seasons and the changes in weather that may occur in Summer (hot), Fall (cool), Winter (cold), and Spring (warm).

Have the students draw a picture of themselves performing some activity during one of these seasons.

●● 2. *Discussion*
Discuss the different seasons and the weather during these seasons. Have students tell which is their favorite season and why.

Point out the geographic and cultural differences in other countries of the world.

Snow is Hot

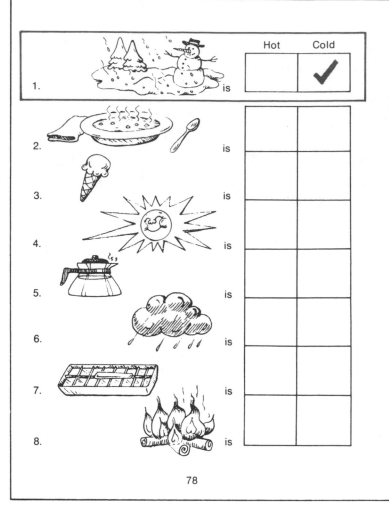

NOTES

_____

_____

_____

_____

_____

_____

_____

_____

_____

_____

_____

_____

_____

_____

78

Snow is Hot

Snow is hot.
> No, it's not.
> No, it's not.

Snow is hot.
Snow is hot.
> No, it's not.

Yes, it is.
> No, it's not.
> No, it's not.
> Snow's not hot.
> Snow's not hot.

Yes, it is.
> No, it's not.
> Snow's not hot.

CHANT GUIDE

PRONUNCIATION:
Practice the pronunciation of **snow, hot, no, not** and the sound of the contractions: **it's, snow's.**

Listen to the intonation pattern of the statement, **Snow is hot,** and the short response, **No, it's not,** expressing disagreement.

STRUCTURE:
This chant provides practice in the *simple present tense,* affirmative and negative, statements: **Snow is hot; Snow's not hot;** followed by the short response: **No, it's not. Yes, it is.**

PRESENTATION:
The accompanying tape provides a model for the presentation of this chant.

NOTES

_____

_____

_____

_____

_____

_____

_____

_____

_____

_____

_____

ACTIVITY GUIDE

TASK:
Using the example as a model, have the students complete the spelling of the name of each animal. The answers follow:

1. dog
2. bear
3. horse
4. rabbit
5. cow
6. donkey
7. goat
8. chicken
9. turkey
10. pig

PRACTICE:

- 1. Review the names of the letters of the alphabet. Have students say the complete alphabet aloud.

- 2. Using the Activity Page, have the students say the name of each animal and then spell it aloud. For example:

  T: What's number 1?
  S: Dog. D-O-G.
  T: What's number 4?
  S: Rabbit. R-A-B-B-I-T.

- 3. Have the students say or write a sentence about each animal pictured on the Activity Page.

ENRICHMENT:

- 1. *Dictation*
  Give a simple dictation drill using the names of all of the animals on the Activity Page. You may also want to include other objects or animals which are familiar to the students, so that they may practice their spelling of these. For more advanced students use complete sentences for dictation.

- 2. *Game*
  Begin the game by asking the class to give you a letter. Cue them for each letter they should shout out, much like the chant and much like a football cheer. Write each letter on the board as the students say it. When the letters spell a word, ask the students, "What does it spell?" Example:

  T: Give me a C.
  S: C
  T: Give me an L.
  S: L
  T: Give me an O.
  S: O
  T: Give me a C.
  S: C
  T: Give me a K.
  S: K
  T: What does it spell?
  S: Clock.

  This may be continued with various words that the students are familiar with, but need practice in spelling.

Give Me a C

	C a t
1.	D ___ ___
2.	B ___ ___ ___
3.	H ___ ___ ___ ___
4.	R ___ ___ ___ ___ ___
5.	C ___ ___
6.	D ___ ___ ___ ___ ___
7.	G ___ ___ ___
8.	C ___ ___ ___ ___ ___ ___
9.	T ___ ___ ___ ___ ___
10.	P ___ ___

80

NOTES

_____

_____

_____

_____

_____

_____

_____

_____

_____

_____

_____

_____

_____

_____

_____

Give Me a C

Give me a **C**.

C

Give me an **A**.

A

Give me a **T**.

T

What does it spell?

CAT

No kidding!
I didn't know that.

CHANT GUIDE

PRONUNCIATION:
Practice the pronunciation of **give, it, what, spell, kidding** and **that**.

Notice the reduction in the sound of the words *give me* (gimme) when they occur in the sentence, **Give me a C;** and the reduction in the sound of the words *what does it* when they occur in the question, **What does it spell?** These reductions are a distinctive feature of American English speech, frequently used by educated native speakers in casual conversation.

STRUCTURE:
This chant provides practice in the *command form* with give me, **Give me a C;** the *simple present tense* question, **What does it spell?;** and the *simple past tense* negative statement, **I didn't know that.**

It illustrates the use of the *indefinite articles a* and *an* as they occur in **a C, an A,** and introduces the exclamation, **No kidding!** to express surprise.

PRESENTATION:
This chant is presented in the style of a football cheer.

NOTES

ACTIVITY GUIDE

TASK:
Have the students look at the picture and make up their own sentences describing what they see in the picture. For example:

I see a little horse. He is waiting for someone. He is standing by a window. There's a child in the window. There are flowers around the window.

The students may wish to add their own drawings to the picture. For example, they may want to draw a picture of themselves riding the horse or sitting in the window or they may want to add other animals or flowers. When they have completed their drawings, they could tell what they have drawn and show it to the class.

PRACTICE:
● 1. Conduct a substitution drill using the structure, **I wish I had a _____.** Use various names of animals to cue the students.

   T: I wish I had a horse.
   T: donkey
   S: I wish I had a donkey.
   T: rabbit
   S: I wish I had a rabbit.

●● 2. *Discussion*
   Have the students discuss the type of animal they wish they had and why.

●●● 3. Have the students practice with the structure, **If I had a _____, I would _____.** Provide several examples and then let each student give his own. Example using the structure:

   T: If I had a big car, I would drive to school every day.
   T: If I had a horse, I would ride in the mountains.
   S: If I had a camel, I would ride in the desert all the time.
   S: If I had ten dollars, I would buy lots of cookies.

   With the students giving their own examples, using this structure, you could continue this into several different discussion groups. Each student would tell his wish or secret fantasy.

ENRICHMENT:
●● 1. *Discussion*
   Have the students tell about the habits of their favorite animal or pet. Ask questions to elicit this information. For example:

   How old is he?
   Does he run fast?
   Is he friendly?
   How big is he?
   What does he like to do best?

●●● 3. *Field Trip*
   If possible, arrange for a field trip to a local zoo. Have the students become familiar with all the names of the animals beforehand, so that they may identify them at the zoo. After the field trip, have them discuss what they liked best and what they didn't like.

The Horse March

82

NOTES

_____
_____
_____
_____
_____
_____
_____
_____
_____
_____
_____
_____

The Horse March

I wish I had a horse.
I wish I had a horse of my own.
And if I had a horse of my own,
that horse would never be lonely.

If I had a horse of my own,
he would stay every day
by my window.

If I had a horse of my own,
he would never be alone.

If I had a horse of my own,
he would stay every day
right by my window.

If I had a horse of my own,
I only know
that horse and I
would not be lonely.

83

CHANT GUIDE

PRONUNCIATION:
Practice the pronunciation of **wish, had, horse, own, lonely, only, stay, day, window** and **never.**

STRUCTURE:
This chant provides practice in the *unreal conditional,* **If I had a horse . . . he would stay;** and illustrates the use of *wish* to express a dream, unrealized at that moment: **I wish I had. . . .**

Notice the use of the *preposition by* to express location, **by my window;** the use of *right* for emphasis, **right by my window;** and the expression, **of my own,** to indicate possession.

PRESENTATION:
The chorus of this song is based on "The Stars and Stripes Forever," written in 1897 by John Philip Sousa. Listen to the accompanying tape for the melody, tempo and style of presentation of this song.

You may want to have the students actually march along with the music and possibly join in with drums, tambourines and other marching band instruments.

NOTES

About the Author

Carolyn Graham, a graduate of the University of California, Berkeley, settled in Turkey for nine years, where she taught English as a Second Language in Ankara and Istanbul. She returned to the United States in 1969, after one year of study in Paris, and joined the faculty of the American Language Institute at New York University.

Ms. Graham is the author of *Jazz Chants*®, *The Electric Elephant*, *Small Talk*, and *Jazz Chant*®*Fairy Tales*, also published by Oxford University Press. She has presented workshops on jazz chanting throughout the world.

She is also a professional entertainer, playing ragtime piano and jazz kazoo in various clubs in New York City under the name of Carolina Shout.

I Found a Cow

I found a cow!
>How?

I found a cow!
>How?

I found a bear!
>Where?

I found a bear!
>Where?

I found a hen!
>When?

I found a hen!
>When?

I found a cow.
I found a bear.
I found a hen.
>When?

I found a hen.
I found a cow.
I found a bear.
>Where?

I found a bear.
I found a hen.
I found a cow.
>How?

I found a bear.
I found a hen.
I found a cow.
>Wow!

45

CHANT GUIDE

PRONUNCIATION:
Practice the pronunciation of **found, cow, how, wow, bear, where, hen** and **when.**

Listen carefully to the intonation pattern of the one-word questions: **How? Where? When?**

Notice the sound of the indefinite article **a.**

STRUCTURE:
This chant offers practice in the *simple past tense statement* using the *irregular verb* **found** followed by the one-word questions: **How? Where? When?**

Notice the repeated use of the *indefinite article* **a.**
The final exclamation word, **Wow!** is used to express a feeling of great surprise or achievement. It may be used sarcastically, at times, to indicate that a particular achievement was not very great.

PRESENTATION:
Maintain a strict rhythmic pattern throughout this chant. The accompanying tape provides a model for the presentation of this chant.

NOTES

ACTIVITY GUIDE

TASK:
Using the example, **pool,** as a model, have the students circle the hidden words in the picture and write them in the spaces provided. The words are: **pool, downtown, she, shell, say, going, go, swim, we, the, to, me, he, is, sign, my** and **in.**

PRACTICE:
- 1. Have the students construct sentences with the hidden words they have just listed. This can be done as an individual or a class practice.

     For a class practice, write each word on a large card. Scramble the cards and place them on the board. Have the students unscramble them and make as many correct sentences as they can. Some examples of possible sentences follow:

     He is going downtown.
     She is going to the pool.
     We swim in the pool.
     The pool is downtown.

- 2. Have the students repeat sentences with *want to* and *be + going to.* Point out as simply as possible that these expressions are treated as a single unit. *Want to* expresses desire, and *be + going to* expresses intent. Each expression is followed by the full form of the verb. Examples follow.

     Want to + Verb
     I want to go downtown.
     She wants to swim.
     They want to fool around.
     We want to play baseball.

     Be + Going to + Verb
     I'm going to watch them.
     She's going to hide.
     He's going to ride his bike.

- 3. Have the students construct their own sentences using *want to* and / or *be + going to.* Be sure that they use the full form of the verb after these expressions in their sentences.

ENRICHMENT:
- 1. *Game*
     Divide the class into working groups of four or five students. Give each group the same list of ten or fifteen words. Make sure the list contains at least two verbs and two subjects.

     Have the groups work for ten minutes trying to construct as many sentences as possible from the list of words. One student can be the "recording secretary" for each group and write the sentences or record them on tape, if you prefer to do this orally. The group with the greatest number of correct sentences at the end of ten minutes is the winner.

Downtown

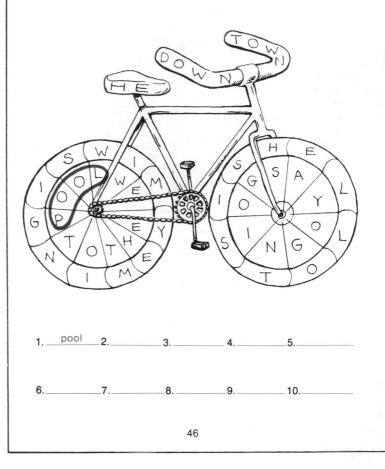

1. __pool__ 2. _____ 3. _____ 4. _____ 5. _____

6. _____ 7. _____ 8. _____ 9. _____ 10. _____

46

NOTES

_____
_____
_____
_____
_____
_____
_____
_____
_____
_____
_____
_____
_____
_____

Downtown

I want to go downtown and fool around.
I want to fool around and go downtown.
I'm going to ride my bike right past the school.
I'm going to jump into the swimming pool.
I'm going to watch the people come and go.
I'm going to say, "Hello, hello, hello!"
If you want to, you can go with me.
We'll have a wonderful time.

47

PRONUNCIATION:
Practice the sound of the contractions **I'm, we're,** and the pronunciation of **downtown, around, fool, pool, ride, right, with, watch** and **wonderful.**

Listen to the reductions in the sound of the words *want to* (wanna), and *going to* (gonna), when they occur in non-final position in a sentence: **I want to go downtown. I'm going to ride.** These reductions are a distinctive feature of American English speech, frequently used by educated native speakers in casual conversation. However, in written and formal communication, *want to* and *going to* are retained.

STRUCTURE:
This song illustrates the use of the *simple present tense statement,* **I want to;** and the *future* with *be + going to* as it occurs in, **I'm going to.**

It also provides practice in the *real conditional,* **If you want to, you can go with me;** and the *future* with *will* to express a promise, **We'll have a wonderful time.**

Notice the use of the expressions **go downtown, fool around, come and go,** and the use of *right* for emphasis as it occurs in **right past the school.**

PRESENTATION:
The music for this song is based on "The Peacherine Rag," written in 1901 by the black American composer, Scott Joplin.

Listen to the accompanying tape for the melody, tempo and style of presentation of this song.

NOTES

_____

_____

_____

_____

_____

_____

_____

_____

_____

_____

_____

_____

ACTIVITY GUIDE

TASK:
Have the students count the number of objects in each drawing and write the numbers in two forms as in the example box: **3 Three.** The guide at the bottom of the page should be reviewed first if the students need counting practice before doing this **TASK.**

PRACTICE:

● 1. *Counting*
Practice oral counting forward and backward with the students who need help with this.

●● 2. *Adding*
Write sample addition problems on the board. Have the students read each problem aloud and supply the answer. First provide the example orally, then let the students continue with other problems.

T: (points to the board) 3 + 1 = 4
  Three and one are four.
T: (points to the board) 4 + 2 = 6
S: Four and two are six.

●●● 3. *Present Continuous Tense*
Present sentences for repetition using various action verbs in the *present continuous tense.* Use pictures illustrating the actions, and have the students pantomime the actions as they repeat each sentence.

T: She's running.
S: She's running.
T: He's jumping.
S: He's jumping.

Once the students have learned the vocabulary in the model sentences, conduct a question and answer exercise by pointing to each picture and asking, "What's he/she doing?" The student's response should be, "He/she is singing." (Or whatever the appropriate action is.)

●●● 4. *Simple Past Tense*
Using the same procedure introduced in **Practice 3** above, give the *simple past tense* of various action verbs by explaining that these activities happened yesterday. Have the students repeat your sentences.

T: Yesterday, she ran.
S: Yesterday, she ran.
T: Yesterday, he jumped.
S: Yesterday, he jumped.

Now conduct a question and answer exercise by pointing to each picture and asking, "What did he/she do yesterday?" The students respond to your cues.

T: What did she do yesterday? (pointing to picture of a girl running)
S: (Yesterday), she ran.
T: What did he do yesterday? (pointing to appropriate picture)
S: (Yesterday), he jumped.

When I Was One

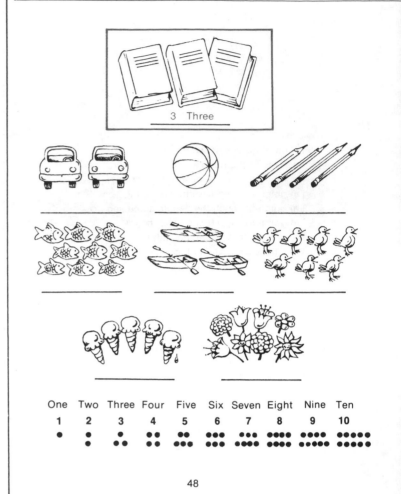

●●● 5. *Discussion*
Using the model questions from the chant, **What did you do when you were _____?**, lead the students into a discussion based on their own answers to what they did when they were one or two years younger.

ENRICHMENT:

● 1. Construct simple dot-to-dot drawings on a ditto using the numbers 1–10 or 1–20. This can easily be done by drawing the outline of a simple animal and then replacing the lines with numbers set up so that the students can reconstruct the drawing if they follow the correct sequence of numbers. (See the more complicated dot-to-dot drawing on page 32 as a general model.)